Orishas

The Ultimate Guide to African Orisha Deities and Their Presence in Yoruba, Santeria, Voodoo, and Hoodoo, Along with an Explanation of Diloggun Divination

Your Free Gift (only available for a limited time)

Thanks for getting this book! If you want to learn more about various spirituality topics, then join Mari Silva's community and get a free guided meditation MP3 for awakening your third eye. This guided meditation mp3 is designed to open and strengthen ones third eye so you can experience a higher state of consciousness. Simply visit the link below the image to get started.

https://spiritualityspot.com/meditation

Contents

Introduction

We're all connected by nature. From shielding ourselves from the rain to searching for a cool breeze when the weather is hot, we all are influenced by Mother Nature and her offspring. But there's more.

Beyond the influence of cold and heat, daylight and darkness influence the supernatural - the unseen realm and forces therein. While our eyes and natural senses help us see and interact with all that is around us, it requires a special form of awakening to perceive the forces of the supernatural. Needless to say, the supernatural holds a great deal of influence over our lives.

Often, we experience things we cannot explain. For some, it's an unexplainable source of constant good luck, but for others, it could be bad luck over and over. Moments of déjà vu, uneasiness, strokes of luck, or sudden, unexplained fear all find their roots in the unseen forces around us. Although we cannot see these forces, we can feel their impact. These forces are none other than the Orishas.

The Orishas are supernatural forces that influence the course of a person's life. Although they're particularly worshipped in the Yoruba religion, they exist and are greatly celebrated in other religions outside the shores of Africa. Religions like Lucumi, Candomble, Santeria, among others, all worship the Orishas for their power - the ability to either bring positive or negative influence into the lives of anyone they please. For instance, Orisha Sango is worshipped for his fierce ability to bring instant judgment to an erring person. He is also worshipped to instill courage into fearful hearts. In the same vein, Orunmila is worshipped to draw wisdom into one's life. Female Orishas like Orisha Osun, Yemoja, Oba, Aje, and Oya are also worshipped alongside their male counterparts. Virtually all the female Orishas are attributed to water elements and help female fertility, childbirth, and women's overall beauty.

While devotees of each Orisha have special knowledge on how to worship the Orishas, it doesn't mean that non-devotees are left out. Non-devotees can also learn the ways of worshipping the Orishas, using the basic applicable steps. This means you need not be a core devotee to worship an Orisha of your choice. You need not have all the mystical knowledge about the Orishas before you can pay homage to or invoke their influence in your life.

The supernatural is limitless, and so are Orishas - they are powerful and uncountable. And they are all available and willing to influence your life if you're willing to call upon them. The choice is yours, and this book is here to guide you. In this book, you'll find truths about the Orishas and also the basic steps you need to take to worship the Orisha of your choice - particularly the major Orishas. One thing is certain, Orisha worship is bound to influence your life greatly, and you determine the energy (positive or negative) you draw from them. May you enjoy your fascinating journey with the Orishas!

Chapter 1: How to Worship the Orishas

A Chinese, a Japanese, and a Korean person may look alike, but they're very different. In their beliefs, languages, and manner of interaction, you can easily determine who is who. While it is said, at times, that these three are distant cousins, it doesn't change the fact that they're different. Just as their languages are different (although often claimed to sound relatively alike), their beliefs are different. In the same vein, while the pantheon gods and goddesses of the Chinese, Japanese and Korean people may possess certain similarities, there are clear differences. Culture determines their identity and manner of interaction.

The Earth is home to diverse people and cultures. Each culture comes with its own beliefs that greatly influence how its people live and interact with others. For instance, a Yoruba man is required by culture to lie face down when greeting an elder. But this is not tenable in other cultures where some are required to kneel, bow, stand a distance away, and pay homage to an elder before approaching him. In all of these instances, culture proves its hold on people's lives.

Regarding culture influencing the way and manner in which its people live, an aspect of culture holds greater influence over the people. This aspect serves as the foundation of all cultural beliefs and is known as the belief in the supernatural. Faith in unseen forces often ensures that the status quo in a particular culture is not tampered with. It is easier for a person of culture to explain away phenomenal occurrences and dictate moral principles based on his/her faith in the unseen forces of his/her culture. For instance, a Yoruba elder would explain the flashes of lightning on a stormy night as the works of Orisha Sango, accompanied by his powerhouse of a wife - Orisha Oya. Likewise, a Yoruba person would be wary of doing certain things forbidden by a supernatural entity. All these serve as the basis for cultural and social interactions.

In the Yoruba culture, supernatural forces abound in their uncountable numbers and are classified as Orishas. These Orishas are greatly worshipped by many, and in return, their virtues and powers are drawn into their worshippers' lives. But who are these Orishas?

How Orishas Came to Be

The beginning of the Orishas is deeply rooted in the Yoruba version of creation. While it is believed in most cultural contexts that all of creation came about due to creation by a Supreme Being or God the Supreme Creator, the Yoruba culture thinks a little differently. It is believed that all of creation was carried out by Obatala, a subordinate of the Supreme Being - Olodumare. Rather than Olodumare carrying out the task, Obatala sought permission from Olodumare and was ultimately granted the task.

According to the Yoruba creation tale, Olodumare, also known as Olorun - the Lord of the Skies - had created two separate spaces, i.e., the skies above and the water below – there was no middle or solid ground. With these two spaces created, Olorun (whose name loosely translates to "the head or chief of heaven") took charge of the sky realm above, while his counterpart Olokun (whose name loosely translates to "the head or chief of the deep waters") controlled the water realm beneath the skies.

Obatala was inspired by a need to create a middle ground - a habitable space for creatures to live in. Hence, he sought permission from Olorun to create a habitable space. Olorun understood what was requested and granted Obatala the permission he sought. But there was more needed.

For creation to take place, wisdom was required. Obatala, who is perceived both as a son and a subordinate of Olorun, went ahead to his elder brother Orunmila (the eldest son of Olorun) for counsel. Orunmila, who doubled as the Orisha of wisdom, prophecies, and divination, responded positively and thought about what would be required to create the habitable space Obatala had in mind. By his powers of wisdom and divination, Orunmila stated that Obatala would require the longest gold chain ever for him to reach the surface of the waters below the sky realm. Aside from the golden chain, Obatala would need to fill a snail's shell with sand from the sky realm, which would serve as the foundation for solid ground. Obatala was also required to go with a white hen, a black cat, and a palm nut - all were to be carried in his bag as he made his descent downward.

Having received counsel from Orunmila, Obatala sought the aid of his fellow divinities - sons and daughters of Olorun, and they responded by offering their gold to him. The collected gold was fashioned into a long chain, while Orunmila supplied the remaining items needed for the downward sojourn. With these items in his bag and the chain fixed to a portion of the sky, Obatala made his descent down the golden chain.

Although the chain was the longest ever created, it could not get to the water's surface. Once Obatala had reached the end of the golden chain and realized there was still a lot more distance to go, he prayed to Orunmila. Orunmila responded by instructing him to pour out the sand from the snail's shell and then release the white hen. Obatala did as he was told. He poured out the divine sand and released the white hen. The white hen landed on the poured sand and began scratching - an act that caused the sand to spread out to different areas. Wherever the sand landed, it turned into dry land with certain spots possessing bigger piles of sand that turned into mountains and hills, while certain other spots with less sand turned into valleys.

Having created dry land, Obatala dropped to one of the hills created and named it Ife, which would eternally be known as the "heart of creation" by the Yoruba people. Obatala moved further and took the divine palm nut out of his bag, and planted it. Once the palm nut touched the ground, it sprouted into a full tree and dropped more palm nuts that sprouted with equal speed. The process of sprouting quickly and dropping new seeds that sprouted quickly continued until the whole area was covered in palm trees and new vegetation. Obatala had succeeded in his mission to create a habitable space.

Settling down from the whole creative process, Obatala dwelt in Ife for a while with the black cat as his sole companion. Over time, he grew weary of being alone and, because of this, he devised a plan. Obatala created clay figures that looked like him and that possessed his physical features. Once these were created, Obatala prayed to his father - Olorun, who breathed on the clay figures, and they became the first living men and women of the Yoruba race.

But, there was an error. While creating men and women out of clay, Obatala took a short rest and got drunk on palm wine. With his eyes still unclear, he continued forging more figures of clay. His drunkenness resulted in the creation of many deformed beings – who also became living humans when Olorun breathed life over them all at once.

Once Obatala realized his error, he made an oath never to drink again and always to protect those who were deformed. Because of this, he is also known as the patron Orisha and protector of all with one form of deformity or another.

Please note that while this is the central creation story according to the Yoruba culture, varying tales are similar. In one tale, Obatala needed to fashion a human companion named Oduduwa who assisted in creation. In another tale, Oduduwa is perceived as being the person who carried out the task of creation after Olorun had blessed him. In all these tales, however, Oduduwa remains the father of the Yoruba people, while Obatala remains the widely celebrated Orisha of creation.

Moving on, with the Yoruba race created, the men and women built huts as they had seen Obatala do, and over time the community prospered. This prosperity drew the attention of fellow divinities - gods who came down to visit and interact with the people. Their visits, interaction, and assistance to the people, eventually had them deified by the people Obatala had created. Summarily, the term 'Orisha' was coined to signify their divine status and capacity to help or influence human lives. Obatala and his fellow divinities were sons and daughters of Olorun - they possessed unique powers and virtues sourced from Olodumare and dwelt eternally in the sky realm.

Consequent to their new name, given by the created humans of the Yoruba race, "Orishas" are deified beings, gods, and divinities worshiped by humans due to their divine qualities and abilities to influence and determine the course of existence, not just for humans but for all of creation. For those who yielded to their counsel and instruction, they offered peace and direction. But for those who did not, they were exposed to terrors that could otherwise be warded off by these Orishas. However, they were willing to embrace any who turned to them for guidance.

Classes of Orisha

According to the Yoruba culture, different Orishas manifest in diverse forms but are unified based on their display of power. To know who Orishas are, the first element to look at is the display of power and how much influence such a being possesses. When displaying power, it is well known for an Orisha to show control over an element of nature viz-a-viz fire, water, earth, air, and other elemental forms such as thunder, lightning, iron, and plants. What's more is that each Orisha is capable of divination, can communicate with other Orishas, and has access to powers that are inaccessible to mere mortals. Based on this, it is easy to understand why Obatala and fellow divinities were known as Orishas.

Going through the pages of Yoruba history and culture, certain people were deified and given the name 'Orisha' without actually being of divine origin like Obatala. These were mostly humans who were either the reincarnation of a preexisting Orisha or were blessed by Olodumare and deified by fellow humans based on their extraordinary exploits. They were capable of divination and possessed divine powers, which they utilized to execute unimaginable feats. As such, they were known as Orishas in their own right.

Because power is a major way to identify an Orisha, for any being or human to be classified as an Orisha, such a being or person must possess extraordinary abilities. Mere hunters and people of divination cannot be deified, largely because they have access to measures of power; such powers are mostly based on self-interest. What's more, such powers are often deemed not powerful enough to be reckoned with by the whole Yoruba community. Hence there is no point in classifying such a person as an Orisha – a custodian of power.

The Yoruba culture, just like every other culture in the world, celebrates people of power and sacrifice. Hence, for a person to be deified, they must possess tremendous power and must have used it for the Yoruba people's good. Sacrifice is a hallmark of an Orisha, and, as such, no mere mortal can be deified without having proven him/herself by power and selfless sacrifice for the good of the Yoruba race.

However, here are the classes of Orisha in the Yoruba culture:

First-Class Orisha

The first-class or category of Orisha is beings of divine origin, e.g., Obatala. They were known as Ara orun – the people of the heavens (skies) – because they came from the sky realm and influenced the Yoruba people and their existence. These were sons and daughters of Olodumare, who was the first and supreme lord over all Orishas. They existed before creation, had access to a limitless supply of power, and could appear in human form.

Some say that this class of Orisha initially visited the Earth regularly in their human forms to interact with Obatala's creation. But over time, they returned to the sky realm and ceased their frequent visits to the Earth. To maintain their influence and help those who called on them, they operated via mortal channels such as dedicated priests, graven images, and certain natural phenomena. Orishas in this class include but are not limited to Olodumare, Orunmila, Obatala, Obaluaye, Esu, and Osanyin.

Natural Elements and Other Spiritual Entities

Another class of Orishas is divine beings with tremendous power but who do not possess human forms. These mostly operate via natural elements and phenomenon and are often deemed subordinates or messengers of Orishas' first class. They are known as Irunmole and only operate on the Earth for a specific purpose and time. Once their mission is accomplished, they return to Olodumare.

In a certain respect, Obatala and his fellow divinities were considered to be Irunmole due to these reasons:

- They're subordinates of Olodumare and often serve as his messengers.

- They returned to the sky realm after their Earthly sojourn and have never visited the Earth since then.

- Due to the vacuum created by their absence on Earth, they maintain their operations and influence on the Earth by oracles, priests, and supernatural phenomena.

The Yoruba culture is rife with major and minor Orishas. The major Orishas are widely known and worshiped in the Yoruba culture, while the minor Orishas are not as widely known or worshiped. Minor Orishas who make up this class are innumerable and are strictly worshiped by a select group of people. Often, they're known as Orisha Idile - household gods, and, as a result, only direct descendants of the family worship them. Their followers are in no way restricted from paying homage or worshipping other Orishas - especially the major or first-class Orishas.

One way, as stated earlier, by which this class of Orishas operates is via natural elements or phenomena. Thus, it is believed in the Yoruba culture that there is a spirit behind every natural element or phenomenon. Hence, prayers must be made when a phenomenon is witnessed, or there is an unnatural stirring of a natural element, e.g., prayers are made during thunderstorms to praise or appease the Orisha behind such a manifestation to avoid destruction. Places where unnatural occurrences are witnessed are turned into sacred grounds that must be respected.

Deified Mortals

The next class of Orishas comprises strictly deified humans. Men, women, kings, warriors, hunters, healers who possessed great powers that influenced the existence of the Yoruba race were granted the divine status of Orisha by their followers and the general Yoruba community as a means of drawing on their virtues and remembering them, despite their departure from the physical/human realm. People like Arabambi Sango were famous kings who were deified by their followers and ultimately became Orishas.

Note, not all powerful mortals are deified. Sacrifice, power, exploits, and overall impact on the Yoruba race determine if a mortal will eventually be deified. Arabambi Sango, for instance, was the fiercest king of the Yoruba people, and he was known for his military and supernatural might. He was known far and wide as the reincarnation of Orisha Sango, the god of thunder, lightning, and fire. This was due to his supernatural ability to breathe fire and summon lightning even without rainfall thunderstorms. Sango ruled with fear and reverence in the hearts of both enemies and subjects alike and was ultimately deified by his followers after his supernatural departure from Earth.

In this same class of Orisha, there are humans just like Arabambi Sango who are known as Orisha due to them being marked by divinities. These reincarnations often serve as channels of expression for the first-class Orishas who no longer visit nor walk the surface of the Earth. They possessed powers and traits akin to the Orisha that marked them and are ultimately worshipped as Orishas in their own right.

How to Worship the Orishas

Before doing anything else, knowledge and an understanding of worship are required. That's the basis for the history and classification of the Orishas. It takes knowing them and how they came about to understand certain truths about them. The truth remains that the Orishas are supernatural beings of great power and influence. They could be called upon to influence a person's life or even judge those who err. However, a careless approach to the Orishas often ends in terror - you may incur the wrath, or another unwholesome result, should you approach an Orisha carelessly. And such carelessness is more often a result of ignorance rather than intention. The Yoruba culture and worship of the Orishas is not a DIY (do-it-yourself) project, and adequate knowledge, experience, and preparation are essential to proper worship of the Orishas.

Remembering that the Orishas operate via physical channels, especially through an oracle (graven image) and a priest, there's an easy way to worship the Orishas. It is simply by visiting the shrine of an Orisha, with an offering in hand and asking that the priest bless you and your offering. Offerings and prayers are important for worshipping the Orishas. Hence you cannot do without them.

Orishas According to Colors

To further explain how to worship the Orishas, they are split into two major categories: Orisha Funfun, the white-themed Orishas who are coolheaded and easy to approach (Orisha Obatala and Orisha Dudu), and the dark or red themed Orishas who are fierce and mostly hot-blooded.

Usually, errors or omissions in the process of worshipping white-themed Orishas are easily pardonable. But such pardon is not available with dark or red-themed Orishas. The difference is in the nature or color of each Orisha. This heavily determines what sacrifice or manner of worship is required.

Note, however, that no Orisha is to be toyed with. Acts of omission may be pardonable when summoning to a coolheaded Orisha, but that is a risk that should not be taken lightly. Just as a dark-themed Orishas can inflict terror or demand a blood sacrifice, a white-themed Orisha can also inflict terror or demand a blood sacrifice. It all boils down to this - blood is the ultimate seal of any sacrifice.

Simple Prayers

While worshipping the Orishas is not a do-it-yourself practice, there are simple and general ways to worship an Orisha. By engaging in simple prayers, you could call upon an Orisha without fear or error. Take, for instance, this prayer offered by Babalawo's when paying homage to Orisha Orunmila each morning:

Orunmila! Eleri Ipin

Ibikeji Olodumare

Ajeju Oogun,

Obiriti, Ap'ijo ikuda

Oluwa mi, Ato'baj'ayeg

Oro abikuj'igbo

Oluwa mi, Ajiki

Ogegg agb'ayegun,

Odudu ti ndu ori emere

Atunori tiko sunwon se,

Amoiku

Olowa Aiyere

Agiri ile-Ilogbon

Oluwa mi: amoitan

A ko mo O tan ko se

A ba mo O tan iba se ke

This prayer can be translated to:

Orunmila! The witness of fate

Second to Olodumare (The Supreme God)

You are much more effective than medicine

You are the great Orbit that averts the day of Death.

My Lord who is mighty to save,

The mysterious spirit who fought death.

Unto you are salutations first due in the morning

Great Equilibrium that controls the forces of the world

You are the One who works to help those with bad luck

Oh Repairer of ill-luck

He who knows you becomes Immortal

You are Lord, the undisposable King

Perfect in the house of Wisdom

Lord who is infinite in Knowledge.

Our failure to know you makes us futile.

Oh, if only we could know you in full,

Then all would be well with us.

Looking at this prayer, it can be deduced this is a matter of praising Orisha Orunmila each day. Trained devotees, priests who are known as Babalawo, engage in this prayer each morning in honor of Orunmila. Once this prayer is said, subsequent prayers (requests) can be tabled before the Orisha, requesting his aid.

Prayer Pattern

The way prayers generally work is that they first make you conscious of whatever entity you're praying to. Then you draw the virtue or unseen energy from such an entity to influence your life. Usually, the content of your prayers determines the influence noticed in your life.

So, to pray to an Orisha, understand the basic pattern of prayers. This pattern goes like this:

- Give praises to your chosen Orisha first.
- State your helplessness and need for the Orisha's help.

- Tell the Orisha about what you need help with - make your requests known.

- Round up your prayer with praises to the Orisha.

Once you have prayed, you may be tempted to doubt, but make sure you don't. Don't give room to thoughts like, "am I sure that worked?" Rather, be patient and keep your mind off the requests you've tabled. It is a general rule in prayers you first believe before you see any results. You first have to believe that an Orisha is potent enough to help you, then believe that your prayers are heard. Let go of doubts and watch for signs (no matter how little) that show that your prayers are being/have been answered.

Ashe

Faith or a strong belief in an Orisha and its supernatural ability is critical to receiving answers to your prayers. It is a foundational concept in many religions, and the Yoruba religion is no exception. As a rule, faith isn't just a matter of strong belief but also professing such belief. Faith in an Orisha must be shown not just via an action (sacrifice) but also via speech. People of faith are known for their daring manner of speaking, and it is a requirement if you want to see results. For example, a Babalawo, when summoning an irunmole - a lower-level spiritual entity or messenger to the Orishas, does not speak with fear but with authority. This is a mark of faith and confidence, and it is crucial when relating to the Orishas.

At times you may need to speak with humility, especially when it comes to petitions or calls for mercy. But at other times, a mark of your faith is your manner of speaking, which is where Ashe comes in.

By translation, Ashe means "so be it" and is a symbol of power and authority. It is the power that allows its user to speak things that relate to reality. An Alaase (user of Ashe) uses his speech to invoke supernatural forces that act based on his/her authority. Imagine a situation where you speak about healing, and a supernatural entity performs the act of healing you just spoke of.

According to the Yoruba religion, Ashe is within everyone. Some say that Olodumare, in blessing the human figures Obatala created, blessed them with Ashe. Like the Orishas who possess and perform wonders via Ashe, Olodumare blessed humankind with Ashe in a similar manner. It should be utilized to communicate with the Orishas and to control the course of one's life. By using Ashe alone, you can determine your destiny and also call upon the Orishas for help.

When praying to an Orisha, remember that you possess Ashe both as a means of authority and to communicate with the Orishas. Use it.

Ebo Riru (Sacrifice)

Virtually all religions agree that sacrifice is important in worship and prayers. Irrespective of the content, a sacrifice remains a sacrifice. Ebo riru loosely translates to sacrifice offered to the Orishas. It is a show of reverence and also guarantees answers to prayers. Depending on the size of your prayer request, your sacrifice could either be as little as a sacrificial meal or as great as a blood sacrifice.

Often, prayer or worship of an Orisha is incomplete without a sacrifice. In a certain respect, all that may be needed as a sacrifice could be kola nut or pouring of wine as a libation to the ground. The Yoruba religion strongly believes in sacrifice as a necessity for drawing on the powers of an Orisha. It helps with calling forth mercy and forgiveness where there is an error, and it also draws other virtues and blessings to the person who offers the sacrifice. It all boils down to this:

"Ebo riru lorisa ngbo."

- Afa'du Owanrin Meji

This translates to:

"Sacrifice is what the Orisha listens to."

Ebo riru cannot and should not be done carelessly. Depending on the situation that calls for a sacrifice, the consequences of error could be grave. A wrong or careless sacrifice is always rejected, and on certain occasions, attracts the wrath of the Orisha to whom the sacrifice was made. Hence, do not carry out a sacrifice all by yourself, especially without first answering these questions:

- What Orisha are you sacrificing to?

- What are the sacrificial meals and items peculiar to the Orisha?

- When and where are you to carry out the sacrifice?

- How do you carry out the sacrifice?

Usually, an experienced priest or devotee could help answer these questions and help you prepare your sacrifice in mind. While sacrifices are important, especially when the purpose of the sacrifice is great, you can still engage in simple prayers and keep your mind at rest.

Divination of Cowrie Shells

To utilize Ashe, knowledge and experience in divination becomes a must. You cannot efficiently utilize Ashe without having some level of experience in the divination of cowrie shells. This form of divination goes by many names but is particularly known in the Yoruba religion as Odu Ifa or Odu Owo Merindinlogun, which loosely translates to the Divination of Sixteen Cowrie Shells. In Santeria, it is known as Diloggun and practiced with strict principles.

The divination of cowrie shells is used to read fates. It allows a diviner access into supernatural secrets of the past, present, and future, and about a given situation. With these secrets, a diviner can ultimately influence fate by offering an alternative or positive change according to what he/she sees when divining.

Chapter 2: Olodumare the Almighty

Every religion and culture believes in a source. It is believed that the Earth was created and is governed by a singular entity existing outside space and time. In most cultures, this singular entity has subordinates created by him to ensure law and order - control over all creation. This is also true of the Yoruba religion that believes in the existence of one supreme entity and Lord over all - Olodumare. By translation, Olodumare means "the owner of the source of creation," which shows that Olodumare is just a manifestation of the Supreme God over all - Olodumare is not all there is to him.

According to the Yoruba culture, Olodumare - as the owner of the source of creation - total control over creation. While he may possess total control, he operates by delegation. Rather than being directly involved in the control of existence, he operates via his sons and daughters - Orishas who possess his virtues, traits, and powers. His sons and daughters are the ones who hold direct control and involvement in matters of creation, and they only operate because of his permission and tremendous power. They report to him.

Since Olodumare operates by delegation - he has no direct involvement in matters of existence. There is no shrine nor priest dedicated to him. According to the Yoruba religion, one can only access Olodumare via another Orisha. If you seek protection, call upon one of the Orishas, and he/she will respond based on your request. Olodumare considers mankind as the choicest of creation and, as such, tasks the Orishas with aiding the destiny of the sons and daughters of mankind. Hence, while you may pray to Orisha Sango for courage in the face of battle, know that Orisha Sango is only responding based on the guiding order received from Olodumare. None of the Orishas operate solely for their own purpose as they live and operate as emissaries of Olodumare to humanity.

Although there is no direct link to Olodumare, prayers can still be made to Olodumare. This happens especially when one either has no idea which Orisha to call upon or the Orishas are unresponsive to a person's call. Here, it is advised to pray directly to Olodumare, who often responds via an Orisha, i.e., he instructs an Orisha to respond. Consequent to the fact that he is the Lord over all other Orisha, none has any choice but to obey him. In all, Olodumare actively controls the realm outside space and time and lets his subordinate Orishas influence the course of creation.

Contrary to popular philosophies, Olodumare exists as the "uncreated creator." He has no beginning, and he has no end. While the laws of time and space may influence humans and their reasoning, it does not disturb Olodumare as he is the source of time and space. He can bend time, space, and natural laws to his will - this can be seen in the demonstration of power by his subordinate Orishas, e.g., the breathing of fire and summoning of lightning by Orisha Sango.

Olodumare vs. Olokun

Often it is said that Olokun is the rival of Olodumare and on an equal footing. While it seems true when you consider Olodumare as Olorun - the Ruler of the Skies, it's not 100% true. Agreed, Olorun rules the skies, while Olokun is the ruler or owner of the waters (both small and great), and it doesn't change the fact that Olokun at best is only on equal footing with a single manifestation of Olodumare as Olorun.

According to the tales of the creation of the universe, particularly the Earth, Olokun was an offspring of Olodumare's action. It so happened that when Olodumare created the universe, the energies present came together in obedience to Olodumare and took form. Amongst the created forms was Olokun, who was born out of the overall mass of hydrogen and oxygen. Olodumare's breath of life impacted every energy, and because of this, Olokun was created. In all, Olokun was the earliest Orisha ever created by Olodumare, and she had Orishas under her command, most being her daughters, who likewise controlled the water element.

Olokun should never be confused for Olodumare or even his manifestation as Olorun. Both rule over different realms and differ in authority. Olodumare rules over everything, including the heavens (skies) and the waters. Olokun strictly rules the waters beneath the heavens, albeit she can influence the heavens' waters in a similar manner. The Orishas submit to Olodumare as father and lord, while select Orishas submit to Olokun as mother and mistress. Olodumare has no equal in terms of power, but Olokun has a rival who rules over the waters in the skies.

In all of this, one thing is spelled out. The created can never be on equal footing with the creator. At best, the created can only express certain traits of the creator.

Olodumare - The Beginning of Creation

Like the Christian perspective of creation, the Yoruba religion believes there was nothing in the big black canvas of space. Olodumare was the only one existing, the only source of consciousness and reason. In his sojourn, he thought about making something meaningful out of the vast emptiness around him. That was the beginning of creation - his thoughts.

Olodumare, who possessed tremendous powers, breathed and gathered vast amounts of energies together - drawing them from all reaches of space. The gathering of these contrasting forms of energy resulted in an explosion of light first before taking on more tangible forms like stars, planets, solar systems, and the entire universe. But there's more.

Recall that before Obatala created dry ground and human figures for Olodumare to breathe upon, there was only the heavens above and the waters beneath. The existence of the heavens and the waters happened after Olodumare had caused the energies present to take form. Some merged to form the waters beneath the heavens.

Out of these waters came a form that can at best be described as a mermaid. It flicked its tail and caused mighty waves on the waters. Then a voice spoke from the form saying "emi olohun omi okun," which loosely translates to "I am the voice of the deep waters." This was the beginning of Olokun, who rules the waters beneath the heavens.

While Olokun dived deep into the waters after speaking, a shadowy figure was left on the surface of the water. It could be described as the residue of Olokun, which ascended above the deep waters. Her presence in the heavens helped form water clusters in the heavens, now known as the clouds. This "shadow" of Olokun is known by many as Yembo Olo'rure and rules over the waters in the heavens.

With the waters and the heavens created, Olodumare made great winds out of his breath to blow across the realm that was eventually the habitation of humankind. Although not giving life, these winds became crucial to the survival of all that had the breath of life in them. Thus, the air (wind) was given a greater purpose than just blowing across the Earth.

Names of Olodumare

To clear things up a little, here are the different names ascribed to Olodumare. Each name is a depiction of how he manifests himself to humanity. Humanity only came to ascribe these names to Olodumare, based on knowledge given to them by the Orishas. These names are often used in praise and also prayers directed at Olodumare himself. At times, the names are also ascribed to certain Orishas to signify the trait of Olodumare they carry.

Since introducing foreign religions such as Christianity and Islam to the African continent, lots of the names culturally ascribed to Olodumare have been syncretized as cultural names for God in these religions. As such, these names are sung, chanted, and repeatedly said in praise of God, who is the syncretized variant of Olodumare, the uncreated creator and source of all of creation.

1. Olorun

This is the manifestation of Olodumare that takes charge of the heavens. As ruler of the heavens and skies, he lords over the abode of the Orishas. The Orishas require his aid if they're to descend to the realm of humankind. Prayers are directed toward the heavens as it is the abode of the Orishas. Once they reach the heavens, only then can Olorun instruct the Orishas to respond to such prayers.

No mortal can get to the heavens in his/her mortal form, as it is strictly for the Orishas. It takes a great deal of sacrifice and a change of form before anyone can access the heavens.

2. Eledaa

This is the creative manifestation of Olodumare. He is the creator and giver of life and all other aspects of creation. The Yorubas believe that everything is tied to Olodumare via this aspect, and, as such, they constantly pray that the creator shields them from bad luck and curses.

3. Elemi

This is a manifestation of Olodumare known for preservation. He is the keeper of life, and everything owes its life to him.

In recent times, this name has been distorted to refer to a person with strong spiritual ties. Here, the person has difficulties in living normally due to being overwhelmed by the spiritual ties present in their life. This kind of person is said to live in between the spiritual and physical realm and often serves as a bridge between the Orishas and mortals.

4. Olu'ase

This name strictly refers to Olodumare as the source of all power and authority. From him, every other Ase is found, and without his Ase, none other can function. Being the source of all Ase, the title Olu'ase - the source and owner of authority, supersedes other variant titles bearing Ase, e.g., Apa'ase - the one who decrees with authority, which is often given to mortal men of high esteem such as kings and celebrated chiefs.

As the source of all authority, Olodumare is likewise prayed to when installing a new king in any Yoruba community. It is believed that the king possesses both divine and mortal authority, and prayers are made both as a show of his divine authority and a submission to the source of all authority, i.e., Olodumare.

5. Olulana

When there is no clear path to take in moments of confusion, Olodumare can be called upon using this name. Olulana loosely translates to "way maker." At times it may be translated to "way-finder," Olulana expounds on Olodumare's all-knowing ability in determining what step to take.

Olumoranokan Eda

It is often said that no one can know the intent of a person's heart, except that person. But the saying does not apply to Olodumare, who is the source of all. The name olumoranokan eda means he knows and is capable of revealing the intent of the heart. No one is outside his scope, and because of this, it is often advised that one thinks only good thoughts and banishes all forms of evil or negative thoughts. This refers to the attributed Olodumare because he is more of a judge of intent rather than action. He bestowed his virtue on Orisha Orunmila, which further taught mankind what is known as Iwa Pele (good character), which begins from within (the heart) and grows outward.

Anyone who wishes to be helped by Olodumare must first cleanse him/herself of evil thoughts or intent. To do this, one must first forgive anyone who has done them wrong and seek to make amends. Purity of heart is vital to be heard by Olodumare, who sees all and knows all hearts' intent. Neither Orisha nor any mere mortal can escape his gaze.

Qualities of Olodumare

It's important to discuss the specifics concerning the traits and qualities in Olodumare which make him stand out from the rest of the Orishas. These traits will help you understand more about Olodumare and influence your mode of approaching him in worship.

1. He is the First Creator

While it is easy to say that Olodumare is the Creator, it is important to state that he is not just a creator like Obatala was. Rather, he is the first creator who created every Orisha and even mortal man with the creative virtue to create even more things. Olodumare is both the first and supreme creator, to whom every other creator submits.

This is depicted in one of the Yoruba tales of creation, where it was said that the world was initially a marshy wasteland with ugly growth here and there. This was after the point when Olodumare created the universe, and the Earth was yet to be fully formed with solid ground, humans, and proper vegetation.

Olodumare and the Orishas lived in the heavens but frequented the marshy wasteland in-between the heavens and the deep waters - this was done via a divine chain. The purpose of visiting the wasteland was mostly for hunting and exercising their divine abilities.

On a certain day, Olodumare summoned Obatala and spoke to him about his desire to great solid ground. To do this, Olodumare gave Obatala a snail shell filled with sand, a hen, and a pigeon and sent him off. Acting upon Olodumare's instruction, Obatala, who doubled as Orisha-nla, descended into the wasteland via the divine chain. Once he'd reached a certain level, he poured the sand onto the marshy ground and lowered the hen to the ground. The hen promptly began scratching and scattering the sand, and by so doing, the sand was spread throughout the marshy surface. Obatala sent word back to Olodumare via the pigeon that he'd finished creating solid ground. Olodumare, in response, sent a chameleon he'd forged to go and inspect the work Obatala had carried out. The chameleon, upon inspection, reported that the ground was solid, but it was not dry enough. Olodumare waited for a while before sending the chameleon back to Obatala. As at this time, the ground had spread far and wide and was perfectly dry.

With the first phase done, Olodumare instructed Obatala to replenish the Earth with all necessary vegetation for life. Obatala, who had been given divine palm nuts, was to plant these which were, in turn, to sprout fees palm trees and replicate over and over until the Earth was full of vegetation. Equipped with the palm nuts which sprouted as Olodumare had decreed, Obatala was able to source palm wine, oil, and fronds with which he created the first shelter on Earth. Although Olodumare gave the instructions, Orunmila aided Obatala with his counsel on carrying out each instruction.

To populate the Earth, Olodumare told Obatala to create human figures out of clay and wait for him. Obatala did as he was told but could not give life to the forms. This was a unique trait of Olodumare as the life-giver (Elemi), and as such, only he could breathe life.

With each batch of humans he molded, Olodumare breathed on them, and they began living, but Obatala was curious and eventually envious of the life-giving power of Olodumare. His envy and curiosity grew to where he made more human figures and hid to watch Olodumare perform his life-giving act. Olodumare, who was all-knowing, knew what Obatala was up to. To handle the curiosity and envy of Obatala, Olodumare put Obatala into a deep sleep so he couldn't tell when Olodumare came around, breathed life into the new batch of human figures, nor even when he left the Earth after he had finished.

2. He is Omniscient

From the legend of creation above, another trait of Olodumare that could be seen is his omniscient nature. He sees everything and knows all things. While many focus on the outward, Olodumare sees both the intents of the heart and the actions of all - no matter how carefully hidden they may be. Because of this, Olodumare is known by another name, "Arinurode Olumoranokan," which means that he is "the one who sees the inside and outside, and knows the intentions of the heart."

3. He is Unmatched

Olodumare, being the first and supreme creator, is on a superior level to every other Orisha. Seeing as he is the source of all things, it is only natural for him to be unmatched. His powers and virtues are exemplary and serve as the basis for every other Orisha, who in turn teaches mankind. Even Olokun, who is, at times, confused as an equal rival of Olodumare, was born out of his acts of creation. She hardly compares to Olodumare's manifestation as Olorun - the Lord of the heavens, who can veto her authority when necessary.

Olodumare is beside himself in all things, the only one whose Ashe is uncontestable. There are no idols dedicated to Olodumare, and that is born out of reverence for his unmatched level. No painting or carving can describe Olodumare, as he is all in all.

4. He is the Immortal Source of Immortality

The Yoruba culture believes that Olodumare existed before the beginning and will continue existing beyond the end. Because he is known as Elemi - the giver and keeper of life, it is only to be expected that he is the source of life cannot die. And this goes to show he is immortal - this can be seen in a Yoruba oriki that says "a ki'igbo iku Olodumare" (we do not hear the death of Olodumare).

Beyond Olodumare's immortality, he is known to be the one who grants the souls of mortal's immortality. In a certain respect, some say that after a person dies, his/her soul returns to Olodumare, who reserves it until a moment of reincarnation (if he so pleases). In the same vein, the Orishas source their immortal and divine nature from him, and that is the only reason they have existed for so long - before man - and will keep on existing.

5. He is Omnipotent

The words "Olodumare l'oba a se kan" are parts of the praises given to Olodumare that mean "he is the king who works unto perfection." Due to his immense power and wisdom, Olodumare works intelligently and ensures that his works and instructions are carried out perfectly. This can also be seen in the tale of creation when he instructed Obatala and sent a chameleon twice to check the work's quality.

Anyone can direct prayers to Olodumare, pleading for him to help ensure that perfection is achieved in any project engaged in. He will respond through Orunmila, who possesses a greater portion of his wisdom, and that will prove helpful. The Yoruba adage summarizes his omnipotence and ability to bless works toward perfection - "a dun'se bi ohun ti Olodumare lowo si, a soro bi ohun ko lowo si" (whatever Olodumare approves is fun/easy to do, but where his approval is absent, such becomes difficult).

Chapter 3: White Orishas I: Obatala and Orunmila

Power comes in different forms. At times it could appear as fierce and destructive, and at other times power could seem as calm and neutral. Just because power seems dormant or inexpressive does not automatically mean there is no power. In the same vein, when power is seemingly expressed calmly, it should not be misunderstood as weakness. Power is dynamic – it can switch from momentary calm to full-on destruction. What matters isn't the potential of power to be either calm or destructive but the wielder of such power. It is often said that a weapon is only as powerful as its wielder, which is not far from the truth. Power likewise is only expressed based on the whims of its wielder.

With the Orishas, they are divided into two categories based on their expression of power. These categories are based on the colors red/black and white. Red/black colored Orishas are noted for their fierce and destructive expression of power, while the white-themed Orishas are known for their calm demeanor. It should be noted that the Yoruba culture does not categorize the Orishas based on the stereotype of good and evil. The colors do not identify an Orisha as evil, neither does it ultimately translate to an Orisha being inherently good. Rather, the colors are mostly based on each Orisha's preferences, and an Orisha determines the color he/she would like to be associated with.

Aside from being a matter of preference, the colors serve as a guide for ritual conduct among worshippers. The red/black themed Orishas often require blood sacrifice and a particular daring among their worshippers during ritual activities. But this is different for the white-themed Orishas, who rarely require blood sacrifice nor fierce display from their worshippers during ritual activities. A white-themed Orisha can require a blood sacrifice, while a red/black-themed Orisha could likewise not require a blood sacrifice – it mostly depends on the nature of what is being requested of the Orisha. In simpler cases, a simple ritual meal (ebo riru) is all that would be required. But the greater the request/need, the greater the sacrifice required.

Among the white Orishas is Obatala, who is first among them and known particularly as Orisha Funfun, Orunmila the source of divination, Aje the source of wealth, Osanyin the source of plant medicine, Yemoja the goddess of the waters, and Oshosi the source of divine focus. Each one of these Orisha is known for calm and ease of being called upon. They offer wisdom, protection, fertility, precision, guidance, and a ton of other positive virtues bound to make life easy and more fulfilling. Some are also affiliated with other light-based colors. For instance, Oshosi and Yemoja are associated with different shades of blue, Osanyin is associated with the greenness of plant life, and Orunmila is often represented with a similar color of green.

Obatala

Obatala is one of the elder gods of the Yoruba culture. He is one of the oldest Orishas in the Yoruba pantheons and is known as the creator of all human forms - who were breathed upon by Olodumare. In certain aspects, he is viewed as the father of all other subordinate Orishas.

Being the one who was tasked with creating the world (Earth), Obatala is honored as the creator of the world, while Olodumare remains the undisputed creator of the universe.

Obatala goes by many paths and is chiefly known for his affiliation with the color white. Orisha Funfun, as he is also fondly known, comes from his name, Oba (which means king), t'ala (which refers to an undyed fabric – a blank canvass on which other colors are cast to represent his varying paths). He is an embodiment of purity, both physically and spiritually, and is considered the light of all consciousness.

To Orisha worshippers, outside the shores of Southwestern Nigeria, Obatala is viewed as Jesus of Nazareth due to him being the savior and protector of mankind. This is aside from the fact that he is the creator of humankind – and the deformed whom he swore to protect.

Like other Orishas that marked or were reincarnated into humans, some say that Obatala was a one-time Oba (king) of Ife. His subjects duly revered him until the point when he lost the throne to Oduduwa (a helper turned rival in certain texts). The tale of his loss of the throne is to this day retold through traditional drama during the Itapa festival in Ile Ife.

While most Orishas have more male paths over female paths, Obatala is known for the existence of dual paths. His paths are equally spread between male and female essences, unlike the Orisha of wisdom – Orunmila, the custodians of Obatala's secrets are mostly female; there are more priestesses of Obatala than male priests.

Paths of Obatala

Just like Olodumare, Obatala expresses himself in different forms known as paths or avatars. These paths serve different purposes and, as such, can be petitioned based on specific needs.

1. Obatala Orisa Aye

This is a female path of Obatala that represents the mystical virtues of females.

2. Obatala Ondo

This is another female path of Obatala. This path is a virgin and lives within rocks at the edge of the sea.

3. Obatala Ayalua

This female path of Obatala is a warrior and destroyer. Obatala Ayalua is a variant and rival of her brother Ayalá.

4. Obatala Alabalashe

This path of Obatala speaks to his children in prophetic dreams. He stands for the past, present, and future.

5. Obatala Olufon

This path of Obatala cannot dwell in the darkness. As such, he needs light at all times – his shrine must always have a source of perpetual light.

6. Obatala Oloyu Okuni

This path of Obatala is the source and owner of the eyes of all humans.

7. Obatala Osha Orolu

This path is known as the king of Eg'wadó.

8. Obatala Okelu

This path is the king of Ekiti and Abeokuta; he lives in the highest of places.

9. Obatala Ana Suare

A male path of Obatala that accompanies Oba Moro. His children cannot throw anyone out of their home nor raise their hands in anger.

10. Obatala Oshalufon

This male path of Obatala gave mankind the ability to speak; he is of the king of Ifón.

11. Obatala Oguiniyan

This male path of Obatala allows no one to see his face.

12. Obatala Obalabi

This path of Obatala is the Originator of Oyó, and it is believed that he is deaf.

13. Obatala Elefuro

A female path of Obatala, the queen of the soil. She is also known as Imolé.

14. Obatala Oba Ayiká

This path of Obatala protects homes. People always ask this path for special protection of their homes and properties.

15. Obatala Oba Malu

This path of Obatala works in the hardest of times to help people overcome obstacles in their lives.

16. Obatala Efun Yobi

This path of Obatala protects his children and those of his enemies. He helps to alleviate pains in the legs and brings harmony to the home.

17. Obatala Alarmorere

This path of Obatala is represented by a saw and hammer of silver.

18. Obatala Orisha Yeye

This is another female path of Obatala and is seen as one of the eldest of the female paths of Obatala.

19. Obatala Ogbon

This path of Obatala walks with his brother Oggán. He oversees the journey of the spirits of Obatala's children when they pass on to heaven.

20. Obatala Aikalambo Male

This path of Obatala is the king of Iká, close to Ibadán. He was born in via Odu Ofun Sa.

21. Obatala Oshereilbo

This male path of Obatala walks with Sango at all times.

22. Obatala Airanike

This path is a warrior who walks with Oshalufón and is called Ajósupato in Arará.

23. Obatala Oyu Alueko

A male path of Obatala that is seemingly selfish, as he wants no other Orisha to have more children than he has.

24. Obatala Orisha Iwin

This path of Obatala is from Owó and is the protector of the palace of Obatala.

25. Obatala Oye Lade

This path of Obatala is a hunter and the king of Ekiti. He always walks with Oshosi, and in the Arará, they call him Bajelo.

26. Obatala Ekundire

A male path from the land of Iyesá accompanies Oduduwa.

27. Obatala Orisha Obrala

This is a young and virile male path of Obatala.

28. Obatala Bibi Nike

A male path of Obatala that constantly rides a horse.

29. Obatala Edegu

This path of Obatala is the king of the lands of Efushé.

30. Obatala Abgany

This path is a teacher of Iyebú. He is blind, lives in water, and is a preserver of life.

31. Obatalá Ayenolú

A male, also known as Yelú and Laguelu, in the city of Ibadán.

32. Obatala Agguidai

A male path of Obatala oversees the messages with Olofi. He has four stones and tools that are sealed, and they may not be touched by the sun, air, or dew.

33. Obatala Orisha Aye

This path of Obatala brought order to the world and gave Orunmila the secret of the Ase.

Oriki Obatala

There are different ways to approach Obatala. Simple prayers can be made to his name, and ritual meals can be placed before his shrine. But one of the easiest to do, which is most recommended for new worshippers and enthusiasts of the Yoruba religion, is to sing praises to the Orishas. These praises serve as a unique form of prayer and are known as 'Oriki.' Each Orisha has at least one oriki dedicated to him/her. Some are available to the general public and sung during festivals dedicated to the Orishas, but other oriki are sacred and only sung by experienced devotees and within closed circles.

Below is an oriki dedicated to Orisha Obatala:

Iba Obatala

Iba Oba igbo

Iba Oba n'le Ifon

O fi koko ala rumo

Orisa ni ma sin

Orisa ni ma sin

Obatala o su n'nu ala

Obatala o ji n'nu ala

Obatala o tinu ala dide

Adiniboiti ri, adupe

Ase, ase, asese o

This oriki translates to:

Praise to the chief of the white cloth

Praise to the chief of the sacred grove

Praise to the chief of the heavens

I salute the owner of the white cloth

It is the owner of white light that I serve

It is the owner of white light that I serve

Chief of the white cloth sleeps in white

Chief of the white cloth wakes up in white

Chief of the white cloth gets up in white

He who creates at will, I thank you.

So, let it be, so let it be, so let it be done.

Another fascinating piece of Oriki for Obatala:

Obatala, the strong king of Ejigbo

Seating at the trial, a tranquil judge.

The king whose every day becomes a feast,

The Owner of the brilliant white cloth.

Owner of the chain to the court of heaven.

Obatala stands behind the people who tell the truth,

The protector of the handicapped,

Oshagiyan, the warrior with a handsome beard.

He wakes up to create two hundred civilized customs.

It is he who holds the staff - Opasoro, the great king of Ifon.

Oshanla (mighty god), grant me a white cloth of my own

You who makes things white,

Tall as a granary, tall as a hill.

Ajaguna, deliver me.

You're the king that leans on a white iron staff.

General Notes on Obatala

- Orisha Obatala was the creator of the Earth and the human race. In certain texts, he was aided by the first man he created - Oduduwa, known as the father of the entire Yoruba race.

- Obatala is syncretized as Jesus Christ of Nazareth. At other times, he is associated with the Catholic saint Mother Mary.

The actual Yoruba culture greatly influences Santeria, Voodoo, and Hoodoo depictions of Obatala. There are only slight variations, and these are mostly seen in the names and oriki. For instance, while the Yoruba culture calls him Obatala or Orisha Funfun, he is known as Oxala, Ochala, Orixala, Orichala, or Oshala in these religions.

- Obatala is worshipped to draw out virtues of peace, purity, and harmony in a person's life. This can be seen from his affiliation to white - a product of his name that talks about adding colors (meaning) to a white canvass (life).

- Obatala will never answer a person with evil intentions. Purity of the heart is important when calling upon Obatala.

- The ritual meals Obatala readily accepts are coconuts, white bread, milk, white rice, and water. These can either be accompanied by simple prayers or by praising him with his oriki.

Orunmila

Orunmila, known far and wide as Orunla or Agboniregun, is a major Orisha of the Yoruba tradition. He is the source of divine wisdom, knowledge, righteousness, and divination forms. His wisdom is so vast that it understands all there is to know about human nature, and he possesses the most effective purification methods. He is the one who founded divination and has his form of divination known as Ifa (the divine wisdom of Olodumare). Ifa divination is only available to a few people who dedicate their lives to learning and diving accurately with Ifa as an oracle. These devotees to Ifa divination are known as Babalawo (priests of Ifa) or Iyanifa (priestesses of Ifa).

According to Yoruba's accounts of creation, he was the Orisha who gave counsel to Obatala on what to do - how to create the dry ground and fashion man from clay. With the creation of man finally done, Orunmila joined his fellow Orishas to visit the earth. He dwelt among the Yoruba people as a priest - the founder of the Ifa divination system, teaching them the ways of Olodumare and how to commune with Olodumare. His powers of divination are always accurate and help to determine the destiny of a person. Popularly known as Igbakeji Olodumare, i.e., the second in command of the supreme God, Olodumare, he is greatly revered in the Yoruba culture, holding a special significance above the other Orishas. Orunmila's special place among the Orishas is mostly because Olodumare bestowed on him the virtue known as Ori (intuitive knowledge). This unique endowment gives him the power to intercede and influence the life and destiny of any person he chooses - and he can do this much more than his fellow Orishas.

Just like every other Orisha, Orunmila came to the Earth and taught mankind the ways of righteousness, wisdom, and divination - ways to call upon Olodumare. Realizing that his sojourn on Earth was not an eternal one, Orunmila knew there was a need to fill the vacuum that his absence would create He foresaw this and gave select people a greater portion of his wisdom, teachings, and skill in divination. These people were to serve as priests in his stead once he departed the surface of the Earth. They were to support his teachings and guide all who sought the wisdom of Olodumare about their lives and difficulties.

The selected people were given the title Awo Ifa which loosely translates to the priest of Ifa. Ifa priests were mostly adult males who had gone through sacred training. The gender limitations were broken over time as certain women showed potential in Ifa divination. Just like the males who underwent training, females chosen by Orunmila were permitted to undergo sacred training before their full initiation. Rather than being called Awo, the females had the unique title of Iyanifa, which loosely translates to mother of Ifa divination.

Duality is a principle in Ifa divination – this refers to the fact that both the male and female are critical to existence and balance - the male cannot exist without the female essence. The female cannot exist without the male essence. Hence, just as there are males initiated into Ifa divination, females were required to be initiated too. Interest and personally being chosen by the oracle play a key role in being initiated.

Odu Ifa

The Yoruba culture greatly honors Orunmila as the greatest priest to have ever walked the face of the Earth. Aside from being an Orisha who existed before the Earth's creation, he also served as a priest of Olodumare during his stay on the Earth. It was during his moments on Earth that he created the divination system known as Ifa.

Odu Ifa referred to a divine collection of stories and prayers possessed by Orunmila and passed down from generation to generation through his chosen priests and priestesses. There are 16 major books under Odu Ifa, and each book has 16 subdivisions of secrets accessible to only the priests and priestesses of Ifa. These 256 Odu Ifa are said to contain all probable situations, decisions and actions, and consequences in anyone's life. With these, the priests and priestesses of Ifa knew and required wisdom to give counsel and guidance to anyone who sought their help. Irrespective of sacrifices that may be required to remedy whatever situation one may find him or herself in, the works of righteousness, also known as Iwa Pele, often saved someone from total damnation.

Although most of the prayers of Ifa divination are sacred and only accessible to the priests and priestesses of Ifa, here is a more generic prayer dedicated to Ifa. It is directed toward the human Ori (spiritual head), which greatly determines a person's destiny.

Ori, mo juba (I honor you and give you thanks),

It is you who is with me through all the events of life.

Ori's l'ori mi (I have a good Ori - head)

Ori ire (good Ori) that links me to Olorun

Ori ire, that is Olorun's essence in me.

Ori ire that is open to receive the blessings that Olorun sends to me

Ori're l'ori mi (I have a good Ori - head),

Ori ire that is open to the wisdom of Ifa

Ori ire that is open to the guidance of Orunmila.

Ori ire that receives assistance from the Orishas - gods.

Ori ire that welcomes and embraces Egungun - the spirits of the dead.

Ori ire that welcomes assistance from Egungun.

Ori're l'ori mi (I have a good Ori - head)

Ori, I beseech you to keep my doors open

Ori, I ask that you always bring me blessings

Ori, I beseech you to always support me in tough times,

Ori, I beseech you to always rejoice in good times with me.

Ori, I embrace you, and I ask that you always embrace me.

Ashe, Ashe, Ashe o (a variant of Amen – so let it be).

Oriki Orunmila

Orunmila Eleri Ipin

Ibikeji Olodumare.

Akeju Oogun,

Obiriti, apijo Iku da,

Oluwa mi, atoibajaye

Oro abiku jigbo.

Oluwa mi, ajiki.

Ogege agbaiye gun.

Odudu ti n du ori emere,

A tun ori ti ko sunwon se,

Amo iku,

Olowa aiyere,

Agiri ile ilogbon.

Oluwa mi amoimotan,

A ko mo o tan ko se.

Aba mo o tan iba se ke.

Mojuba akogda,

Mojuba aseda

Akoda ti n ko gbogbo aiye ni Ifa

Aseda ti n ko gbogbo agba n'imoran

The translation is:

Orunmila, the witness of fate,

The second in command to Olodumare (Supreme God).

You are far more effective than medicine.

You are the one who averts the day of death.

My Lord, the almighty to save.

The mysterious spirit that fought death,

Unto you salutations are due first in the morning.

You are the equilibrium that adjusts the forces of the world

You are the one whose exertion it is to reconstruct the creatures of bad luck.

You are the repairer of ill luck.

He who knows you becomes immortal.

Lord of the King that cannot be deposed.

Perfect in the house of wisdom.

You are the lord who is infinite in knowledge.

By not knowing you in full, we – your servants are futile.

If only we could know you in full,

All would be well with us.

I praise the first created

I praise the creator

The first created who teaches the whole world the divination of Ifa

The creator who teaches the elders wisdom.

General Notes on Orunmila

- Wisdom and righteousness are the hallmarks of Orunmila. His devotees are expected to walk in the righteousness of heart and actions.

- Orunmila is a diviner that can foretell the destiny of anyone. Where there is uncertainty or evil ahead, Orunmila can be called upon for wisdom on how to avoid such evil. He can rewrite destiny, but only in agreement with the person concerned. Such a person needs to be ready to work according to instructions. Otherwise, there will be no change in destiny.

- Variations in the worship of Orunmila in Santeria, Voodoo, and Hoodoo religions are mostly based on the blend between actual Yoruba and the predominant language in places such as Cuba, Brazil, and Latin America, where these religions are predominant. As such, Orunmila is mostly known as Orula in Santeria.

- Orunmila is worshipped so that a person can walk in wisdom and depth of perception. This way, a person isn't just sensitive to happenings, as a person who calls on Orunmila is further endowed with the wisdom on how to live, act or react, to forestall problems.

- A true devotee of Orunmila must be righteous, i.e., clear of bad intentions and actions. Forgiveness and slowness to anger or picking offense are crucial to a devotee.

- While perfection is seemingly impossible, devotees of Orunmila are encouraged to grow, taking each step at a time to live righteously.

Chapter 4: White Orishas II: The Water Gods

The Yoruba culture has a unique reverence for women. This stems from the duality belief that the Earth comprises both male and female energy. Both energies exist in harmony to ensure balance. It is believed that the creation of the world was incomplete without the input of female energy. Out of the universe's creation, Olokun was formed and became a crucial part of the creation of thriving life forms on the Earth. Obatala could not carry out Olodumare's instruction without first receiving permission from Olokun to create the solid ground on the surface of the waters she controlled.

It is believed that women possess a dual nature of calm and destruction – depending on whichever is entreated. A woman's touch can either bring about calm and prosperity, or it can cause total downfall. In virtually all cases, it is the lives of men that are greatly influenced by the virtues that flow from women. This shows that the male energy, which is most fierce, requires female energy's calming virtues. Since the female energy is mostly calming and dynamic, most of the female Orishas are affiliated to the color white and are predominantly controllers of the water element. Osun, for instance, was known for her beauty and calming influence over Orisha Sango, and her virtues are implored to help women become more desirable to their husbands. Female Orishas are predominantly white Orishas, and that goes to depict not just their calming virtue but also their beauty, prosperity, and creativity.

Recalling what was said about the two types of Orishas, female Orishas are also capable of great terror. Orisha Oya is a typical example – as a matter of fact, she is mostly associated with the color red, which symbolizes her ferocity. She is the only female Orisha actively engaged in her husband's military might – she reinforced Orisha Sango's powers and assisted him actively in military campaigns. Her thunderstorms always made it easy for Sango to summon lightning upon enemies, and as such, victory was guaranteed in most cases. Orisha Oya shows that female Orishas are not all about calm and beauty but are also a fierce power that must be reckoned with.

Olokun

Just as every Orisha is sourced from Olodumare, the first creator, every female Orisha – particularly those who control the water element are born out of Olokun. Olokun is the overall patron goddess of the deep waters and the Orishas who rule over the waters. She is the source of all the waters on Earth and is praised for her ability to minister good health, prosperity, and fertility to those who call on her. It is believed that none of the children of Olokun can suffer barrenness, as she is believed to be the source of fertility. Based on the belief of duality, Olokun is seen as both female and male, but she predominantly operates as a female Orisha.

According to the tale of creation, Olokun had always governed the waters after she was born out of Olodumare. There was no cause for alarm nor disagreement as she was in harmony with Olorun. When Obatala carried out the creation of solid ground, it turned out to be a breach of her authority. She hadn't yet given her consent, and he'd already begun his descent – in a certain context, as he had already poured the sand out of the snail shell, and the solid ground had already formed.

Angered by the encroachment on her territory, Olokun, who resided in the deepest parts of the waters, rose violently to the surface and began submerging everything in water – the first humans that existed were at risk of being drowned, and they desperately cried to Obatala for help. Realizing his error and being unable to pacify Olokun, Obatala sought counsel from Orunmila, who instructed him to fashion the longest chain he could ever create and use it to subdue Olokun. After this, Obatala sought the aid of Ogun, the god of iron, to help with the creation of the chain. This was quickly done to ensure all was not lost to Olokun's rage.

With the long chain, Obatala battled with Olokun taking her back to her territory in the deepest parts of the oceans where he chained her down, thus reducing the effects of her temper on the waters. One thing was certain, Obatala was acting on Olodumare's instructions, and although Olokun's temper was seemingly justified, she could not go against Olodumare's command. Because of this, her reacting in anger to Obatala executing Olodumare's instruction was seen as rebellion. Eventually, Olorun had Olokun pacified. An agreement was reached, and the waters were restrained from crossing into the land. Hence, no matter how far the water moved, it was made to recede to its source in honor of the agreement.

In all the stories about Olokun, her outbursts often caused great manifestations in water bodies around the area. Some say that during her reincarnation as the senior wife of Oduduwa, she was engaged in a heated rivalry with one of her subordinate wives, and that led to the birth of the Atlantic Ocean far away.

Oriki Olokun

Olokun aje ti aye oba omi

Omi nla to kari aye

Osele gbe senibu omi ti koni momo

Gbogbo eni ti waje

E je ka kori si ile Olokun

Sanle aje

Iya eni to l'aje

Iya eni to l'aje

Ogbugbu ni so oni so boji

Alagbalu gbu omi

Alagbalu gbu omi

Eni ajiki

Eni ajike

Ai ri di Olokun

Ao mo bere re

Aje pe gbogbo omi

E fi ori fun Olokun gbogbo odo

E fo ori fun Olokun oba omi

The translation is:

The owner of the waters and prosperity – the Queen of the realm of waters

The great waters that cover the Earth

A wonderful ocean that has no end

Whoever seeks wealth, let them go to the house of Olokun who has abundant wealth

Mother of uncountable wealth

Mother of uncountable wealth

Waters without end

Waters without end

The one we greet when we wake

The one whom we cherish

No one knows the source of Olokun

No one knows her beginning

Prosperity calls unto all the waters

Let the waters bow to Olokun

Crown Olokun as the Queen of the waters.

General Notes on Olokun

- Olokun is the source of all water-based Orishas. She is the mother of Yemoja, Oya, Osun, Aje, and every other minor Orisha affiliated with the water element.

- Olokun operates via duality. She is predominantly female and manifests with the male energy at certain points.

- Santeria, Candomble, and other Yoruba-oriented religions in the diaspora recognize Olokun as a powerful Orisha, but just like Olodumare, she is not directly worshipped.

- Olokun is the source of wealth – a virtue she bestowed predominantly on her daughter Orisha Aje who is worshipped directly.

Yemoja

Yemoja is an Orisha that controls waters and is also known as the second in command of Olokun – she is the eldest daughter of Olokun. According to Santeria, she has been syncretized as the Catholic saint, the Virgin Mary. This is also replicated in the Afro-Cuban areas where she is known as "Our Lady of Regla." Virtually all the names borne by Yemoja point toward her affiliation with motherhood and the Virgin Mary. Names like Yemaya, Madre del Agua, La Sirene, among others, demonstrate this. They point to her being a protective mother who is sourced from the waters.

As an Orisha, Yemoja is protective of her children – all of humanity - and she shares in their joys and sorrows. When the Yoruba Empire fell, and many were taken out to sea to be sold as slaves, some say that her devotees cried out to Yemoja, the mother of the waters, to console them of their loss and help them find strength and courage during turbulent and strange waters. Yemoja responded by bringing calm to the sea waves, keeping the hearts and minds of the people strong until they were able to reach land and continue the Yoruba tradition.

Besides being a mother to all, Yemoja has a soft spot for her female children (women) and offers them the cure to infertility. An infertile woman only needed to offer sacrifice to Yemoja, and in return, Yemoja would offer one of her eggs to the woman to encourage fertility. Yemoja takes charge of all things that pertain to women – especially the areas of childbirth, nurturing, love, and healing.

As a mother of the waters, Yemoja is mostly calm and associated with blue and white colors. She is responsible for the calm waves on the rivers and seas, but she can also rise in anger, and that can cause a tempest. Here, devotees promptly offer sacrifices to appease her and restrain the tempest. Where the tempest persists, prayers are made to ensure that life is not lost to the tempest.

Due to the vastness of the sea and the fact that it is the resting place of uncountable riches, it is believed that Yemoja owns the riches hidden deep in the waters. Because of this, her symbol includes cowries sewn into clothes of white or blue colors. She is often prayed to by fishermen to bless their voyage and ensure they rake in bountiful fish harvests.

Like her mother, Olokun, Yemoja is often illustrated as a mermaid. But generally, she is seen as a beautiful Nubian woman walking on the surface of the waters. The moon is also a symbol of Yemoja and can be seen in most illustrations about her.

Paths of Yemoja

34. Yemoja Yembo (Yemu)

This path of Yemoja is the mother of all Orishas and is the source of the crown of Yemoja. She is often said to be Oduduwa in female form.

35. Yemoja Ibu

This path of Yemoja is married to Orisha Aganyu, and they often meet on the riverbank.

36. Yemoja Ibu Oleyo

This path of Yemoja was born in Odun Ogunda – Iroso. She is a lover of fish and hens and is always dressed in light blue.

37. Yemoja Ibu Olowo

This path of Yemoja was born in the Odu Odi-Iroso. Yemoja Ibu Olowo is the owner of all the riches trapped in the depths of the waters.

38. Yemoja Ibu Okoto

This path of Yemoja was born in the Odu Merunla – Iroso. She is said to live in conch shells.

39. Yemoja Ibu Asesu

This path of Yemoja is the patroness Orisha of the ducks, swans, and geese. She is the revered messenger of Olokun and requires patience when being called upon.

40. Yemoja Akere

This path of Yemoja lives in the deepest parts of the ocean and is born of the Odu Odi-Ojuani.

41. Yemoja Oro

This path of Yemoja works with egungun (masquerade spirit) and operates mysteriously.

42. Yemoja Achaba

Born out of the Odu Osa Mesan, this path of Yemoja talks about her royalty and is often represented as an anchor. Some say that she is the one who finds shelter in the anchors.

43. Yemoja Okute or Okunte

This path of Yemoja was born of Odu Ogunda Meji and served as the wife of Ogun. She is a warrior – patroness of the Amazons and is a hard worker.

44. Yemoja Mayelewo

This path of Yemoja is the favorite daughter of Olodumare. She was born in Odu Irosun Ofun and lives at the bottom of the ocean. Her chief virtue is that of stability.

45. Yemoja Ibuagana

On this path, Yemoja is the wife of Orisa Oko and is born of the Odu Iroso-Metala. While she is said to be beautiful, she has seven lumps on her abdomen and has one leg thinner than the other.

46. Yemoja Atarawa

This path of Yemoja is said to be the owner of treasures found both in the ocean and on land.

47. Yemoja Ibubunle

This path of Yemoja is born of Odu Eye'nle Meli. She lives atop reef rocks and has symbols such as a hook, sword, seashells, and paddles, among others.

48. Yemoja Ibu Akinomi

This path of Yemoja dwells in the water's waves and is born of Odu Eye'nle Odi.

49. Yemoja Ibuconla

This path of Yemoja is born of Odu Odi-ejila. She builds ships and is often seen as a poet or muse for poets.

50. Yemoja Ibuina

This path of Yemoja is a warrior and doesn't shy away from disputes or wars. She is born of Odu Osa-ogunda. Her preferred meat is that of carp and goats.

51. Yemoja Ogunayibo

This path of Yemoja is born of the Odu Marunla-Ogunda and is known for her large breasts. She is a warrior who works with Orisha Ogun and is the patroness Orisha of older women.

52. Yemoja Ogunosomi

This path of Yemoja works with Ogun and Sango. She is a warrior who lives on the surface of the waters and also climbs mountains. She is born of the Odu Iroso-obara.

53. Yemoja Ibunodo

This path of Yemoja dwells in rivers and is symbolized with a silver chain.

54. Yemoja Yemase

This path of Yemoja has a mighty crown on which seven ritual cowries, machetes, and axes are hung. These are further supported with a boat and an arrow from Orisha Oshosi.

55. Yemoja Ibualaro

This path of Yemoja can be described as the Orisha of life and death.

Oriki Yemoja

Agbe ni igbe're ki Yemoja ibikeji odo

Aluko ni igbe're ki'losa, ibikeji odo

Ogbo odidere I igbe're k'oniwo

Omo at'orun gbe 'gba aje ka'ri w'aiye

Olugbe rere ko, Olugbe rere ko, Olugbe rere ko,

Gbe rere ko ni olugberere

Ase!

Translation:

It is the bird that takes good fortune to the Spirit of the Mother of the Fish - the assistant to the goddess of the Sea (Olokun)

It is the bird Aluko that takes good fortune to the Spirit of the Lagoon - the Assistant to the goddess of the Sea (Olokun)

It is the parrot who takes good fortune to the Chief of Iwo

Children are the ones who bring good fortune from Heaven down to the Earth

The Great One who gives good things, The Great One who gives good things, The Great One who gives good things,

Give me good things from the Great One who gives good things.

So, let it be.

General Notes on Yemoja

- Yemoja is one of the seven most worshipped Orishas in Brazil

- She is perceived as the guardian Orisha of fishermen and sailors during shipwrecks. Tons of shipwreck survivors testify to being pulled to safety by an unknown force and also having visions of mermaids and sweet voices while struggling to survive in the water. This has been attributed to Yemoja as the mother of "fish children" - mermaids who instruct her children to rescue shipwreck victims.

- Yemoja is seen as "Our Lady of Seafaring" in Salvador - a Catholic symbol for safety on water voyages.

- Yemoja accepts offerings like flowers, porcelain dishes, mirrors, jewelry, and other feminine items.

- Festivals attributed to Yemoja are held on these dates, February 2, September 7, December 8, and 31.

Osun

Osun, the most beautiful and favorite queen of Sango, is an Orisha that works hand in hand with Orunmila – the Orisha of wisdom and Ifa divination. Osun, also known as Ochun or Oxum in Latin America, is one of the daughters of Olokun and is also a water-based Orisha in the Yoruba pantheon. She is the goddess of the Osun River that flows between Osun and Ekiti in Southwestern Nigeria. She aids fertility, love, beauty, and the overall appeal of women. She is also active in divination, just like Orunmila.

According to Yoruba mythology, Osun was the female Orisha whose energy ensured that all that was created was beautiful. Some say that when Olodumare decided to create the world, the male Orishas began the creative process without the female Orishas' influence. The world lacked form and beauty – a special power solely attributed to the female Orishas. Osun, who was to lead the female Orishas in influencing the course of creation, was ignored, and, because of this, she went to her partner Sango for help. Sango, who was known and feared among all other Orishas, forced the other Orishas to listen to Osun and accord her the same respect they accorded him. It was only then that they listened to Osun, and the world began to take shape beautifully. As it is said, a woman's touch is what makes things beautiful.

Paths of Osun

56. Osun Ibu Kole

This path of Osun works with a vulture. She serves as a watcher over homes and eats whatever sacrifice is brought by her vulture.

57. Osun Ololoridi

This path of Osun is a fighter and a proponent of revolution. She welcomes change borne out of struggles.

58. Osun Ibu Akuaro

This path of Osun likes eating with her sister Yemoja and is known to her children by a secret name.

59. Osun Ibu Ana

This path of Osun is the owner of drums.

60. Osun Anani

This path of Osun is argumentative. To invoke this path is to prepare to defend one's case before help is released.

61. Osun Ibu Yumu

This path of Osun is famous for her beauty. She has no suitor due to her being deaf. It is uncertain if her deafness is figurative or literal.

62. Osun Ibu Odonki

This path of Osun lives where the stream is born. She is the essence of the mud of the river and the owner of the streams.

63. Osun Ibu Ogale

This path of Osun is an old fighter that hates being disturbed.

64. Osun Ibu Akuanda

This path of Osun was born in the Odu Ikafun and is known for freeing Sango after Oya imprisoned him.

65. Osun Ibu Adesa

This path of Osun is a preserver of royalty. Her name means that she is the one who has her crown well secured. She owns a faithful peacock.

66. Osun Ibu Alade

This path of Osun works hand in hand with Eshu.

67. Osun Akuase Odo

In this path, Osun was said to be stillborn and works with spirits - especially those of the dead.

68. Osun Ibu Bumi

This path of Osun has a personal Eshu that she works with.

69. Osun Ibu Eleke Oni

This path of Osun is blessed with a good character aside from her beauty.

70. Osun Ibu Itumu

This path of Osun is a patroness Orisha of the Amazons. She is a warrior who rides an ostrich into battle.

71. Osun Ita Timibu

The path of Osun is a communal leader and only manifests at night.

72. Osun Ibu Aremu Kondiamo

This path of Osun is born of the mountains. She lives on an Ifa divination table.

73. Osun Ibu Semi

This path of Osun lives in areas around the rivers.

74. Osun Ibu Fonda

This path of Osun is a warrior who died at war.

75. Osun Ibu Odoko

Osun works with Orisha Oko in this path; she is known as a farmer in this case.

76. Osun Ibu Awuayemi

This path of Osun speaks via Odu Oyekun Meli – she is blind and walks with five bronze canes and a horse.

77. Osun Ibu Idere Lekun

This path of Osun dwells in caves and always rejoices anytime the waves hit the ocean reefs. She wears a mask to hide her deformed face. This is the only path where Osun is seemingly ugly.

78. Osun Ibu Inare

On this path, Osun lives on wealth and is the daughter of Ibu Ana.

79. Osun Ibu Agandara

This path of Osun was born in Odun Ikadi and is always found sitting in a chair with a lock.

80. Osun Oroyobi

On this path, Osun is gifted with precious sands by Olokun. She prefers salmon as her favorite ritual meal.

Oriki Osun

Iba Osun sekese,

Latojuku awede we mo

Iba Osun Olodi,

Latojuku awede we mo.

Iba Osun ibu kole,

Latojuku awede we mo.

Yeye kari,

Yeye 'jo,

Yeye opo,

O san rere o.

Mbe mbe ma.

Yeye, mbe mbe l'oro.

Ase.

The translation is:

Praise to the Spirit of Mystery,

The Spirit who cleanses me inside out.

Praise to the Spirit of the River,

The Spirit who cleanses me inside out.

Praise to the Spirit of Seduction,

The Spirit who cleanses me inside out.

Mother of the mirror,

Mother of dance,

Mother of abundance,

We sing your praises.

Remain (exist), exist always Mother,

Exist always in our tradition.

So, let it be.

General Notes on Osun

- Osun worship is done on the bank of rivers – especially the Osun river.

- Osun only accepts ritual meals placed in white or yellow dishes. Where a sacrifice is not accepted, it remains in the same spot. But when accepted, the water's tide will pull the sacrifice into the water.

- Osun provides wealth and beauty, which is shown in her symbols such as gold and copper. She is often depicted as a beautiful woman and only offers her virtues for wealth and beauty to women.

- Osun is syncretized with the Catholic saint known as "Our Lady of Charity," which is a reminder of her being a symbol of love and beauty. Just like her sister Yemoja, she is also depicted with the moon.

- In Santeria, Osun is known as Ozun. Other varying names are accorded to her in Hoodoo, Voodoo, and Candomble (where she is known as Nkisi Ndandalunda).

Chapter 5: Other White Orishas

The Orishas are known for their immense power, but how they express their powers determines what category of Orisha they fall into. For those who are associated with the color white, these are predominantly calm and easy to be entreated. But be wary that you do not incur their wrath due to carelessness or ignorance. Every Orisha is a force to be reckoned with – never to be toyed with.

As it is said, there is more than a countable amount of Orishas existing. Some are only worshipped and recognized in households, while others are known on the far-off shores of Africa. Despite how much an Orisha is known, one thing is certain – such an Orisha is an embodiment of power and influence over devotees' lives. The Orishas can also touch Non-devotees, but that depends on the circumstances – it could be an answer to the prayer of a devotee or an unexplainable stroke of divine intervention. Consequently, the White Orishas are more important than the majors listed in the preceding chapters. There are many more whose knowledge is hidden in cults and households, but in all – what matters is that a White Orisha can be asked for help without a necessary threat to life, and this is best done aided by a devotee. Simple prayers and offerings just in reverence of an Orisha are welcomed, but you need to give the right offering, say the right prayer and chant the right praises if you want to be accepted.

When in doubt of what offerings to give, do not make an offering – you shouldn't give an offering at all and then risk wrath due to error and ignorance. One thing is certain. You can never go wrong when giving praises. A simple greeting, such as "Orisha Aje mo juba" – Goddess of wealth, I greet you, is a good start. You can always chant rich praise or give a worthy offering after you've done the needful research and preparation under the guidance of an experienced devotee.

With all that said, let's get down to other White Orishas worthy of mention:

Oba

Orisha Oba is one of the daughters of Yemoja (conversely an offspring of Olokun) and a major Orisha in the Yoruba pantheon. Unlike most Orishas, with different names in Santeria and other Yoruba-oriented religions, Oba is known far and wide only by her name. Still, she is syncretized as the Catholic Saint Catherine of Siena.

Although she is not as widely known as her sister Orisha - Osun and co-wife - Oya, she is a water goddess in her respect. She is the patroness of River Oba that flows from Igbon in the Yoruba region of Nigeria. According to Yoruba legend, she served as the senior wife of Sango but was to a great extent the least loved. Oba is forever at enmity to Osun, who tricked her into cutting off her ear and feeding it to Sango - to have their husband love her more. While there are variations in Oba's tale in Santeria regions, her rivalry with Osun is the most prominent. Oba's hatred for Osun was born out of the trick played on her where she asked Osun for help in getting Sango to love her more. Osun, who was the most loved, rather than helping her co-wife (which is seemingly understandable as she wanted no rival to hold Sango's heart), resorted to trickery. She informed Oba that Sango was in love with her due to her sacrifice - she cut off her ears and fed them to Sango. Although Oba did not believe this initially, she was convinced when Osun told her there was nothing to worry about since the ears always grew back fast.

Yielding to the outrageous counsel by Osun, Oba cut off her ears to feed her husband. However, rather than endearing her to Sango, this singular act made him furious to where he exiled her from the palace. Some say that Oba exiled herself out of shame in other variations to the story - she did not want her husband to see her without ears, neither did she wish to give her rival a chance to mock her continually.

From the legend, one thing is clear, and that is the fact that desperation was the undoing of Oba. But that, to a great extent, is understandable. She was the eldest wife who had to bear the excesses of a virile husband - Sango. His subsequent marriage to Oya and Osun was hurtful to her. With the new wives' presence, she gradually receded into the background where she hardly commanded the attention of Sango, and with this change, her desperation was fueled.

Consequent to her being tricked by Osun and being the least loved among the wives of Sango, she became revered as the patroness Orisha of exploited hearts. Oba is said to console hearts that have been broken or are lovesick.

Like her fellow Orisha and wife, Osun, Oba controls bodies of water and is a daughter of the Yemoja. Her rivalry is seen to this day at the confluence of the River Oba and River Osun – the consistently turbulent crashing of water at the confluence of both great rivers is seen as both Orishas fighting eternally.

While devotees sing the praises of Oba, such praises are not commonly known. In the same vein, prayers and unique details concerning sacrifices and days of worship are mostly known by devotees – a pointer to the fact that Oba is mostly shrouded by the shadow of her co-wives' shadow Orishas, Oya, and Osun.

Aje

Aje is one of the daughters of Olokun – the Mother of the Waters and Seas, and because of this, she has a strong command of the natural element of water, just like her sister Yemoja. However, in

Yoruba mythology, Aje is strictly known as the principal Orisha of Wealth. In Santeria, Orisha Aje is known as Aye, who at other times manifests as Aye Shaluga, and she works with Osun in blessing her children with wealth.

All matters of business, money, and wealth are ascribed to Orisha Aje, who is often called Aje Olokun, i.e., Aje, the daughter of Olokun. Market women, traders, and even hunters who sell bush meat pray to her before selling their items. A common Yoruba greeting among traders says, "aje a wa o," and it is a short prayer to Orisha Aje to bless their businesses - it simply means "there will be sales." This greeting that doubles as a prayer to Orisha Aje, also draws the virtues of wealth or opportunities for wealth toward whoever says the prayer. It is both a communal and personal means of growing wealth.

Aside from being the Orisha of wealth, Aje goes by a principle of working to earn. A lazy person cannot pray to Aje, and only those who work can pray to Aje to bless their work and make them wealthy. It is often said there is no food for a lazy man. This means that only those who are diligent in business can discern when Aje creates an opportunity to provide wealth. This is an added confirmation that hard work will surely pay off. Aje can only bless the work of your hands, not hands folded in laziness.

To offer sacrifices to Aje, you must include one or more of the following: bananas, ekuru - a special type of corn cake, honey, or beans. Aje likes sweet meals and will bless based on the sacrifice offered.

Nana Buluku

Nana Buluku is an Orisha that appears as an older woman. She goes by many names in Santeria, Voodoo, Candomble, and other Yoruba cultural religions. She can either be called Nana Buruku, Nanan-Bouclou, and, in certain contexts, Nana Buluku. Among the Catholic Saints, she is identified as Saint Anne and Our Lady of Mount Carmel (the mother of the Virgin Mary). She is a white-themed Orisha who also operates fiercely. She can be likened to

Orisha Oya, who is a fierce Orisha of the water element. However, Nana Buluku controls the earth. In her possession are her traditional ileke, casha, and ja which are unique to her. She accepts offerings like tobacco, garlic, rum, cypress, coconuts, coffee, tomatoes, and shrimp, particularly on her feast day, the 7th of July. It is advised that you do not ask for anything from Nana Buluku without being an initiate. At best, non-devotees can only honor her with their offerings or seek the assistance of an experienced devotee to help with their request. Nana Buluku detests offerings placed in iron plates or bowls. This is due to her enmity with Orisha Ogun, who offended her greatly. Because of this, she commanded her children never to come to her with any item of Ogun the Orisha of iron.

As an Orisha, Nana Buluku is worshipped majorly in Ghana rather than in the Yoruba regions of Nigeria. This stems from her being the supreme deity of the Fon people of Dahomey, who share ties with the Yoruba race. She is the patroness Orisha of women - a fierce protector who will not allow her children to be abused. As a fierce protector, Nana Buluku offers her aid in healing, pregnancy, justice, and rape. She even aids women in terminating unwanted pregnancies - especially those caused by rape. Nana Buluku is often termed stubborn because she never changes her mind.

Nana Buluku lives in the swamps and prefers being alone. At best, only her children or grandchildren may stay with her. According to legend, Ogun tried invading her swamp but lost his battle due to his metal rusting. Due to his futile invasion attempt, Ogun irritated her by being abusive to his wife - Nana Buluku detests domestic abuse of both women and children. Because of this, she responds angrily, even willing to eliminate an unrepentant abuser.

Nana Buluku is the mother of the divine twins who maintain balance over all creation, Lisa the sun god, and Marwu, the moon god. In a certain context, she is the mother of Babaluwaye, who is the patron Orisha of healing. Due to her affiliation with the earth and nature, Nana Buluku detests any actions against the earth. Poaching, wanton felling of trees, and pollution of all forms can incur the wrath of Nana Buluku.

Nana Buluku possesses immense wisdom and healing virtues, which she often grants to her devoted children. Some say that for one to become a daughter of Nana Buluku, she would have to give up the ability of childbirth while helping others with fertility issues.

Osanyin

Osanyin is an Orisha of the Yoruba pantheon who goes by Osain, Ossaim, or Osoin in Yoruba-centric religions such as Santeria and Candomble Voodoo, and the likes. He is syncretized as the Catholic Saint Joseph and is known for healing and herbal medicine. All forms of herbal medicine are sourced from Osanyin, who has divine knowledge about all plants in existence. He is an Orisha of divination in his own right and works – at times–with Orunmila.

Herbalists under Osanyin are known for their in-depth knowledge about plants and their medicinal attributes. It is often said that while science takes long to find a cure, herbalists under Osanyin only need to look at the plants and make the cure. This is a pointer to the fact that Osanyin isn't just a healer of spiritual illnesses but also an active healer of natural illnesses. At times illnesses are self-inflicted, but that makes little difference to Osanyin, who heals without discrimination.

For herbalists to heal, they resort to drawing on the powers of Osanyin via his iron staff (it is said to be the storehouse of Osanyin's powers). The staff, which is known as Opa Osanyin, and at other times called Opa Erinle, is used during the process of divination and is often placed on the floor beside the sick. It is designed with a crown on it upon which sit 16 small birds looking inward and a larger bird in the center looking outward. According to Yoruba belief, the staff symbolizes the dominion of good over evil and supernatural forces. Factually speaking, the smaller birds represent witches capable of transforming into birds to aid the healing process being carried out by Osanyin, who is the large bird in the middle. It should be noted that the birds on the staff possess various meanings. While some perceive the bigger bird as Orunmila, others perceive the smaller birds as messengers from Ogun symbolized as the bigger bird, who aid the healing process of Osanyin.

A proverb is common to herbalists under Osanyin, and it speaks of the duality of the powers of leaves. Some say that "the leaf which can cure you, can also kill you" Hence, care must be taken when using plants for medicine.

Oshosi

Oshosi is the Orisha of the forests. He controls all life and wealth in the forests and is the one who permits hunting. In Candomble, he is known as Oxóssi, while in Santeria, he is known as Ochosi and is syncretized as the Catholic Saint Hubert. He is depicted as a man with a bow and arrow and with a stag standing beside him - these are likewise the symbols of Oshosi. In other contexts, Oshosi is syncretized with Saint Sebastian in Rio de Janeiro and syncretized as Saint George in Bahia.

It should be noted that the Orishas were syncretized with Catholic Saints by the Yoruba people, who were sold as slaves. It was a means to cover up their religious practices from slave masters who detested such practices. Thus, wherever the enslaved Yoruba people were moved to, they syncretized the Orishas based on Saints with similar attributes such as Orisha. Hence, Oshosi, for instance, is syncretized with three different but similar Saints - his worship is made on the celebrated days of such Saints viz-a-viz 20th January for Saint Sebastian, 6th June for Saint Hubert, and 23rd April for Saint George.

Oshosi is known as the source of food or meat and is known for his swiftness and wisdom in hunting. He accepts mostly animal sacrifices such as goat, guinea fowl, and pig. He also accepts cooked maize, yams, and black beans, among other vegetables.

Oshosi is greatly worshipped in Brazil due to the presence of the Amazon and is often seen as a lone Orisha who comes and goes into forests in a bid to consult plants. Eshu, Osun, Ogun, and Oshosi are the Orishas known as Warriors in Santeria and Candomble. Some say that Oshosi was the only Orisha to ever declare war on Ogun due to a disagreement. Normally, Ogun starts wars due to him being the Orisha of war, but in this case, he was challenged by Oshosi. Although the battle was fierce and long, neither was defeated and because of this, a truce was formed. The truce eventually grew to be a long-standing friendship due to the respect they had for each other's fearsome powers.

Ori

Each person is believed to have their own deity, called Ori, who controls destiny. To entreat Ori into granting good fortune in a person's life, cowrie shells are used to design a sculpted oracle for the Ori.

Ori, who is otherwise known as Ori Inu (the Head Within), is a major factor in what happens in a person's life. Fate is decided in the shrine or dwelling place of Ori. Ori is the foundation upon which human personality dwells. While some are born with certain personalities, Ori can be influenced to be changed or influenced for the better. A person with bad manners is bound to get into trouble. But Ori can be appealed to for a change of such a personality. However, this can only work alongside the person's willingness to shed such personality traits.

Ori is further worshipped as a means of spiritual balance and guidance in each person's life. While consulting Ifa is good when a person wants clarity and knowledge about his/her destiny, Ori is personally available to all. Before consulting Ifa, Ori is readily within reach of consultation. Ideally, Ori is consulted first before Ifaas; at times, what Ifa reveals will require a person to appease Ori first before further actions are carried out.

The potency of Ori varies in each person. Some closely commune with their Ori, while some are ignorant of Ori's existence. Hence there is confusion and no clear direction for life. Regardless, each person can develop a cordial relationship with his/her own Ori by engaging in prayers and greetings to Ori. Think of it like blessing your day each morning and night. This way, whatever is being said to Ori - the prayers or greetings ultimately draw in virtues to a person's life. Whether such virtues are positive or negative is determined by the individual.

Chapter 6: Dark Orishas I: The Trickster and the Warrior

The dark ones are often seen as harbingers of destruction and evil. But that is not entirely true. Agreed, they are expressive in a temper and exude an aura of intimidation; the dark Orishas, or those predominantly associated with the colors red and black, are not all shades of evil. Orishas such as Ogun, Sango, Oya, Esu, and Aganju, among others, are known as dark Orishas due to their ferocity. But it doesn't mean that they are evil. At worst, Esu is known as the Orisha of mischief – and his mischief is often directed toward erring persons. Orisha Ogun doesn't just start wars – there is always a reason for every war. The dark Orishas are known summarily for their terror, which is a fundamental reason for them being worshipped and celebrated greatly.

Esu

The best description that can be given to Esu La'olu Ogirioko is none other than a trickster. As an Orisha, he can be likened to Loki of the Norse pantheon due to his mischievous nature. Pronounced Eshu and known as Exu in Latin America, he is the Orisha of trickery, mischief, crossroads, death, and chaos. He is also the Messenger (Elegba) to all other Orisha. Some say that Esu manifests in 256 paths when acting as Elegba the Messenger to all other Orisha - according to Ifa divination. However, Ocha divination says that Esu only manifests in 101 forms. He could either manifest as Esu Aye, who worked hand in hand with Olokun, or he could work with Sango and Oya devotees as Esu Bi - a fierce path that appeared either as an old man or young boy. Esu Bi is known for protecting and playing with children - particularly twins. At other times, and most often, Esu works with Osun, where he takes the path as Esu Laroye - a diminutive and talkative oracle.

Out of all the 256 paths of Esu, the path known as Esu Odara is the father of all other paths of Esu. Legend has it that the paths of Esu were created during his fight with Iku (the spirit of death). After a prolonged battle, Iku struck a seemingly fatal blow by slicing Esu into two. However, out of the halves sprang two new Esu. Surprised but unmoved, Iku kept cutting down Esu, and Esu kept on increasing, birthing new replicas until the battlefield was overfilled. Iku, who tired of the battle, turned and fled, leaving Esu to deal with his clones.

Aside from his fight with Iku, Esu, when he served as Elegba to other Orishas, must manifest in forms unique to each Orisha he is working with. It follows, he created new forms of himself that would take on different appearances fitting to each Orisha he worked with. Thus, it is often said that Esu is as uncountable as the Orishas of the Yoruba religion. Some say that Esu is the divide between the Orishas and evil forces or demons known as Ajogun. While the Orishas counter the actions of the Ajogun in the lives of mankind, Esu stays in between both parties as a mediator. He is both a messenger to the Orishas and the leader of the Ajogun. The Ajogun serve as his emissaries of mischief and judgment. Out of 201 Ajogun, Esu has eight chiefs. They are Iku, the spirit of death who he fought with before birthing his new paths; Arun, who is the spirit of all sickness; Egba, who is the spiritual source of paralysis; Epe, who is the spirit of all curses; Ewon the spirit of imprisonment; Oran who is a troublesome spirit; Ofo who is the spirit of misfortune and grave loss; and Ese who is the spirit of error and all other forms of the problem.

Depending on the path Esu decides to take, he must never be toyed with as the slightest error from anyone will make him unleash havoc through his unending supply of mischief. In a certain context, Esu is said to carry a bag where he stores his mischief. At times the bag is depicted as big, and at other times it's very small, but whichever size it is, the bag is said to be limitless, and hence Esu can never run out of tricks.

When engaging Esu, one requires patience and wisdom to get the best of Esu, who likes playing on intelligence. Esu helps make decisions, striking a balance between good or sensible decisions and bad or foolish ones. As the Orisha of crossroads, he offers help when confusion sets in. Good decisions can be made through Esu, and these will cause success, blessings, and ease, but where bad decisions are reached, Esu doesn't hesitate to reel out the consequences trapped in such terrible decisions. This ultimately points to the fact that although the Orishas influence the course of a man's life, free will to make decisions and take actions is solely controlled by man. You are made or marred by the decisions and actions you take. It is only wise to seek the wisdom of the Orishas before carrying out your plans.

Paths of Esu

81. Esu Laroye

This path is one of the youngest of Esu. He is behind every door and loves joking around, playing pranks, and is overly mischievous. He is a good friend and messenger of Osun.

82. Esu Lagu'na

This path of Esu is known for his strength and is the patron Orisha of Egungun (masquerades which are the spirits of the dead).

83. Esu Bi

This path of Esu is always seen at crossroads. He breeds discord, doubts, and misfortune on erring persons. His lessons are always taught via painful and, at times, deadly mischief. Where the required lesson is not learned, he doesn't hesitate in dishing out more punishment. Here, Esu can either be your best friend or your worst enemy – you need to be wise when dealing with him.

84. Esu Anaki

This path of Esu is seen as a female. Esu Anaki is an enforcer of law and order among the numerous paths of Esu. She instructs each path on how to commune with humans and also the other Orishas.

85. Esu Aina/Bara Aina

This path of Esu is a messenger too and works hand in hand with Orisha Sango. He is the one who opens the way for Sango when he goes to battle.

86. Esu Arerebioko

This path of Esu is the path that works with Ogun. Esu Arerebioko accompanies Ogun whenever he goes on adventures or hunts in the forest.

87. Esu Aye

This path of Esu walked the seashores. This Esu knows all that we want. Aye also means the world – hence he knows the secret places of riches and mundane pleasures common to humankind.

88. Esu Elegbara

This path of Esu is a carrier of good fortune and blessings to his followers.

89. Esu Alaketu

This path of Esu sits on the outskirts of the town of Ketu in Africa. He is a wise man that brings fortune to the town.

90. Esu Afra

This path of Esu is from Arara, the land of Dahomey. Esu Afra is a close friend of Asojano. He is received when one receives Asojano.

91. Esu Ana

This path of Esu is the owner and path to the sacred drums. He opens the path for communication between the sacred drums and the Orishas.

92. Esu Ashikuelu

This path of Esu lives at the entrance of the marketplace. He is a great negotiator and is used to settle issues relating to money.

93. Esu Bara Layiki

This path of Esu is carefree and loves dancing or partying.

94. Esu Dako

This path of Esu resides in the forest. He knows the herbs and how to hunt.

95. Esu Alboni

This path of Esu resides high in the mountains.

96. Esu Ayeru

This path of Esu is the messenger of Ifa.

97. Esu Aroyeyi

This path of Esu guards the entrance to Olofi's castle.

98. Esu Ode/Ode Mata

This path of Esu walks alongside Ochosi in the hunt.

99. Esu Owo

This path of Esu guards all the riches of the world.

100. Esu Beleke

This path of Esu loves to play as a child. He loves to dance and brings good fortune to those who deserve it.

101. Esu Eluufe

This path of Esu is aged and wise. He doesn't like to be disrespected under any circumstances. He grants wisdom to those who seek and are worthy.

Oriki Esu

Esu,

Esu odara,

Esu la'olu ogirioko

Okunrin ori ita

A jo langa lau

Arin lanja lalu

Ode ibi ija de mole

Ija ni otaru ba d'ele ife

To fi de omo won

Oro Esu, to akoni

Ao fi ida re lale

Esu ma se mi o,

Esu ma se mi o,

Esu ma se mi o.

Omo elomiran ni ko lo se.

Pa ado asubi da

Na ado asure si wa

Ase o!

This translates to:

Divine Messenger,

Divine Messenger of Transformation,

Divine Messenger speak with power.

Man of the crossroads, dance to the drum,

Tickle the toe of the drum.

Move beyond strife,

Strife is contrary to the Spirits of the Invisible Realm.

Unite the unsteady feet of weaning children

The Word of the Divine Messenger is always respected

We shall use your sword to touch the Earth.

Divine Messenger, do not confuse or hurt me,

Divine Messenger, do not confuse or hurt me

Divine Messenger, do not confuse or hurt me.

Confuse or hurt the child of another (instead).

Turn my suffering around

Give me the blessings of the calabash.

So, let it be.

General Notes on Esu

- Esu is the Orisha of crossroads and can help with indecision

- Esu, being a mischievous Orisha, does not like dull people. He plays a lot on intelligence and will often reward intelligence greatly.

- Esu is both a messenger and a chief. He serves other Orishas but stands as the chief of the Ajogun.

- Esu is the first to receive sacrifice before any other Orisha in a festival or ceremony – he is the messenger and must be petitioned before carrying a sacrifice to a particular Orisha.

- Esu is known as Eleggua in Santeria. He is also known as Elewa – the handsome one, and Elegbara, among other names in Yoruba-centric religions in the diaspora.

- Due to his mischievous nature, he is known as Exu in Candomble, a variant name for the devil.

- Esu is a witness to the past and the future – he needs no form of divination to recall the past or foretell the future. The past is a culmination of decisions and actions, just as the future is determined by decisions and actions – and he governs these decisions and actions.

- Olodumare blessed Esu with the divine keys to every sacred door, so he is deemed the first among other Orishas.

Ogun

Ogun Lakaaye, also known as Ogum in Latin America, is the Yoruba god of iron and war. Incarnated as a powerful warrior who became the first Ooni (king) of Ife after the exit of Oduduwa, he is greatly respected among the Yoruba people and the Haitians, Brazilians, Cubans, and in certain parts of West Africa. He is the patron god of blacksmiths, metal workers, craftsmen, and warriors who wield metal weapons.

According to Yoruba mythology, before Ogun became reincarnated into a man, he was the Orisha known for creating pathways. With his sword, cutlass, or ax in hand, Ogun cleared the path for other Orishas to find their way to Earth – particularly Ile Ife where Obatala dwelt. With his faithful companion – a dog, Ogun is often praised as the first Orisha to have come to the Earth, as every other Orisha had to wait for him to pave a path for them to follow.

Regarding his incarnation into a mortal man, Ogun was the first Ooni of Ife, a powerful one who commanded respect from subjects and enemies alike. When a person disrespected him, Ogun had the person executed swiftly by beheading.

Some say that Ogun Lakaaye was one of the most active and responsive Orishas even after departing from Earth. Being the god of war, rather than dying from a self-inflicted wound, he descended into the ground with a vow to respond quickly to anyone who called upon him. Acting on his promise, anytime there was a threat of war or raiders came to disturb Ire Ekiti's peace where he dwelt, the people only needed to run to his grove and call his name for help. Once he was called upon, Ogun would sprout out of the ground in a fierce whirlwind with his sword in hand and rush into the community where he would butcher anyone who looked threatening. It was advised that every indigene of Ire Ekiti stay indoors lest they got cut down by Ogun during his vengeful attacks on invaders.

Ogun came to the aid of Ire Ekiti's people for years until his power was eventually abused. Some say that Ogun stopped surfacing when a group of drunks summoned him from his grove, claiming that there was war in the land. As usual, Ogun sprang into action and killed everyone in sight. As it turned out, he realized he had killed innocent but drunken people instead of invaders.

Angered by their folly, Ogun vowed never to resurface again since they had toyed with him. But mercifully, he was willing to intervene through the wisdom and might he bestowed on Yoruba warriors.

Ogun Worship

Ogun Lakaaye being the patron Orisha of blacksmiths, hunters, and warriors, is represented by an iron (sword), a dog, and palm fronds. He is often revered as the Orisha of truth because anyone who swore by Ogun (kissing a piece of iron and calling on Ogun) would be forced to tell the truth or risk being struck down by him.

Being the god of iron, Ogun worshippers utilize all sorts of iron items during festivals and celebrations of Ogun. Items such as knives, local Dane guns (for hunters), iron chains, swords, blacksmith equipment, wrenches are displayed during the Ogun festival.

Although Ogun had a dog as his companion, sacrifices made to Ogun are incomplete without the beheading of a dog held apart by its head and hind legs. Ogun being the patron Orisha to hunters, mostly calls for sacrifices of bush meat. However, he will receive other forms of sacrifice such as kola nuts, Emu Ogidi (palm wine), palm oil, cockerels, salt (due to its iron content), snails, yam, alligator pepper, and water.

Paths of Ogun

102. Ogún Onile

The owner of the land. He is called Ogun Onile due to his nature as an explorer. He is praised for discovering new territories, animals, and even water bodies. This title means he was the first to come to an uncultivated place and settle in and was the first to work the land.

103. Ogún Alagbo or Alagbede

This path of Ogun is a blacksmith and serves as the patron Orisha of all blacksmiths. He is a hard worker who tirelessly works day and night. Due to his nature, he is anti-social or rude as all his time and attention are focused on his work rather than holding conversations.

104. Ogún Meji/ Ogún Bi

This path of Ogun has two faces. One is the representation of a good and hardworking parent who is peace-loving. The second face, however, is extremely violent, destructive, and bloodthirsty.

105. Ogún Arere

This path of Ogun is strictly a butcher.

106. Ogún Shibiriki

The creator of all things metal and is also called the murderer. He is always jealous of Sango and fights over the love of Yemoja. He is fierce, brave, and of great courage. Fighting is second nature to him.

107. Ogún-Kobukobu

This path of Ogun is known as the foreman. He is often seen with a whip in his hand.

108. Ogún Aguanile

This path of Ogun is a conqueror. He is the one who lords over mountains and newfound lands.

109. Ogún Adaiba

This path of Ogun is a warrior who shows love via his machete.

110. Ogún Jobi

This path of Ogun is a warrior who constantly lurks in bushes and ambushes his prey and enemies. He is violent and doesn't hesitate to react with destruction.

111. Ogún Adeola

The warrior who became king. He wears his crown with honor and reigns with wisdom, overseeing his people's safety and welfare.

112. Ogún Já

This path of Ogun is known for violence and is a fierce warrior. He is said to savor a blood bath in place of bathing in water. He feeds on dogs and causes a lot of arguments and violence if left without attention.

113. Ogún Oloka

A title associated with Ogun being the owner of the lands, and he is known as a farmer. He works the land and owns the fields and what is grown. He is praised for his good harvests and is also known as Olorukó, Olokuló.

114. Ogún Aroyo (toye)

This path of Ogun is known for being violent and impulsive. He is hot-tempered and highly irrational. He serves as the palace's best guard, as he reacts swiftly to what he perceives as a threat.

115. Ogún Onira

This path of Ogun is associated with rain, mud, and the murky waters of the river. This name was given to him because, in this path, he was king of the town of Ira.

116. Ogún Onire

This path of Ogun is known as a conqueror, warrior, and general of armies. He was once the king of the city, Ire.

117. Ogún Oké

This path of Ogun is known as the owner of the mountains and also goes by the names Afanamule and Ogún Ogumbí.

118. Ogún Aladú

This path of Ogun declared war on Yemoja at different times.

119. Ogún Valanya or Ogún Valenyé

This path of Ogun is known as the tiller of the ground.

120. Ogún Niko

This path of Ogun serves as an assassin.

121. Ogún Olode

This path of Ogun is the head of the hunters.

122. Ogún Soroka

This path is known as 'the highest speaking' path

123. Ogún Wari

This is another path of Ogun characterized by violence and destruction.

Oriki Ogun

When venerating Ogun, this Oriki (praise chant) is usually rendered:

Ogun Lakaaye o!

Ogun alara ni n gb'aja

Ogun onire a gb'agbo

Ogun Ikole a gb'agbin

Ogun gbengbena oje igi ni'imu

Ogun ila a gb'esun isu

Ogun akirin a gb'awo agbo

Ogun elemono, eran ahun ni je

Ogun o, makinde ti n dogun leyin odi

Bi o ba gba Tapa a gb'Aboki

A gba Ukuuku a gba Kemberi.

This translates to:

Ogun Lakaaye o!

Ogun manifests in seven paths

Ogun of the town of Ilara is the one who accepts a dog for atonement

Ogun of the town of Ire will accept a ram for atonement

Ogun of the town of Ikole will accept a snail for atonement

Ogun of the town of Gbenagena drinks tree sap for atonement

Ogun of the town of Ila accepts yam seedlings for atonement

Ogun of the town of Akirin accepts the fleece of rams for atonement

Ogun of the town of Elemono eats tortoise for atonement

Ogun o, the brave that wages war with aliens/foreigners

He will destroy either Nupe or Hausa

He destroys alien/foreign people and will destroy Kanuri too.

General Notes on Ogun

- Ogun is the Orisha of iron and all forms of war. Great wars and minor disputes are sparked by him and always interest him.

- While Ogun is known for warfare, he is also known for his wisdom and a prosperous ruler in different contexts.

- Ogun is the patron of discovering and conquering new lands.

He predominantly requires meat sacrifice, especially dog meat. But he welcomes other meals such as kola nuts, Emu Ogidi (palm wine), salt, and the likes. Blood is a predominant requirement of Ogun.

Chapter 7: Dark Orishas II: Shango and Oya

Among the hot-tempered, dark Orishas lies the power couple Orisha Sango and his fierce wife, Orisha Oya. They're predominantly warriors whose powers complement each other, thus guaranteeing them certain victory in battle - for the most part.

Sango

Sango is a fiery Orisha of the Yoruba pantheon known for his predominant color, red. In a certain respect, white or black is added to a red cloth in honor of him. Sango (pronounced Shango), who is known in Latin America as Xango or Chango, is the Orisha of thunder, lightning, and fire and evokes fear in the hearts of any who dare to defy his might. As an Orisha, he is the embodiment of male power, virility, and "merciless" justice.

According to Yoruba history, Sango was initially an Orisha before he was reincarnated into Arabambi, the son of Oranmiyan. His maternal grandfather sensed that Arabambi had been marked by the Orisha of thunder and lightning, and hence he gave him the appendage Sango in recognition of his true identity as the reincarnation of Orisha Sango. Arabambi Sango grew to be a fierce young man known for taming and playing with leopard cubs.

As a strong young man, Sango danced only to the beat of his own Bata drum (he had a dedicated Bata drummer who followed him wherever he went – to festivals, battlegrounds, fighting challenges, etc.). However, due to his principle of never dancing to the sound of other drums, except his own Bata, he drew jealousy from fellow dancers and spectators who mocked him for dancing only to the Bata drum. Arabambi, who was hot-tempered – a personality trait drawn from the Orisha within him, sought for the power to breathe fire. His quest to breathe fire proved successful as his mother's people from Tapa aided him.

Over time, Arabambi Sango grew stronger and was crowned as the third Alaafin (king) of Oyo. He took over the throne of Oyo from his elder brother Ajaka who was deemed a weakling. According to Yoruba history, Oyo suffered from raids carried out by warriors of Owu, an inferior Yoruba kingdom. All this happened during the reign of Ajaka, and it got so bad that the king himself was captured by the raiders – a humiliating experience for Yoruba royalty as they would rather die than be taken captive. It took the might of Sango to rescue Ajaka and restore Oyo as a military powerhouse in the Yoruba kingdom.

Sango's reign was one of might and terror as he engaged in countless wars, which he constantly won due to his fearsome nature and command of the natural elements thunder, lightning, and fire. His command of the elements was obtained from a charm known as edun ara, which his mother's people had bestowed on him. Sango was known for his sacred double-edged ax and had three wives Oya, Oba, and Osun, who became powerful Orishas of the Yoruba pantheon. Oya, the third and most powerful wife, is greatly respected by Yoruba warriors for her active participation in her husband's military campaign. Being the goddess of mighty winds and storms, her powers complemented him greatly, making it easy for him to summon thunder and lightning.

Although Sango brought about great prosperity and expansion to the Yoruba kingdom - no one would dare attack Oyo while he was the Alaafin -his fierce temper became his undoing - he ended up striking his palace with lightning. This act caused the wildfire to spread beyond the palace. An uprising of the people ensued against him, and they demanded he stepped down as Alaafin. In response, Sango left the city along with his chiefs and members of his royal cult known as Baba Mogba.

Some say that Sango hung himself on an Ayan tree in the region of Koso in some accounts. But this has over time being declared false by Sango's devotees. According to them, a usurping general Gbonka ambushed Sango and his party while he was leaving Oyo. However, Sango, who was grieved and unwilling to fight, turned and disappeared into thin air. He later appeared in the sky with fury and summoned lightning upon Gbonka, his ambush party, and the peddlers of rumors he - Sango had hung himself. Hence, he is revered as Olukoso, which means the king did not hang.

Sango is greatly worshipped in Yorubaland. His followers possessed a peculiar protection in that they could easily summon the wrath of Sango on anyone who wronged them, believing him to mete out due punishment. Seen as one of the most powerful Orisha in the Yoruba pantheon, Sango worshippers are governed by a unique code. Just like the fearsome Orisha, his followers braid their hair and attach cowries to it. While they may offer foods of worship such as bitter kola, amala, and gbegiri (mashed beans) or soup, Sango followers are forbidden from eating cowpea as that would incur the wrath of Ogun, the god of iron, and Sango's patron Orisha.

Paths of Sango

124. Sango Obadimeyi

This path of Sango signifies the relationship between Sangó and Aganju, his twin brother. Sangó and Aganju must be attended to equally.

125. Sango Obakoso

The title that Aganju was given after ascending the throne of Oyó, which meant the return of Sangó.

126. Sango Bum

In this path, Sango is seen as the son of Obatala and Yemoja.

127. Sango Dibeyi

This path of Sangó depicts the relationship between him and the children he bore with Osún; these children are known as Ibeyi.

128. Sango Alafi

This path of Sango is linked to royalty, government, legislation, law, justice, and superiority. Sangó Alafi is well respected for his authority and a great sense of justice.

129. Sango Arira

In this path, Sangó is the owner of the rains. He is present in times of rain, puts an end to the drought, and brings peace.

130. Sango Olose

In this path, Sango is the owner of the double-edged ax and holder of power. Sangó Olosé is a great warrior and strong character, and his words were never doubted.

131. Sango Kamukan

Sangó Kamúkan works with egun and has dominion over life and death.

132. Sango Obara

Sango is poor and raggedly dressed in this path, yet his word is the law, and he never lies. The house touched by the beam of Sangó Obara will be deserted and cursed.

133. Sango Jakuta

Sangó Jakuta is a path of Sangó, which means 'the stone thrower.'

134. Sango Ko So

Sangó Ko Só is a path of Sangó, which means "he did not hang himself." This relates to the events that occurred after the death of Sangó, the fourth Alaafín of Oyó.

135. Sango Bara Lube

This path of Sangó was the master of divination before Orunmila.

136. Sango Olufina Kake

This path of Sangó is the owner of the ceiba tree. Some say that he is the creator who sets fire to the roads.

137. Sango Obalube

Sangó Obalúbe is a path of Sangó, which means "The king who attacks with the knife." It was in this path that Sangó met his wife, Oyá.

138. Sango Obaluekun

Sangó Obaluekun is the appellation of Sangó, which means "the king who hunts leopards."

Oriki Sango

This is one of the best Oriki sung in honor of Sango and is best enjoyed with the beat of Bata:

Sango Olukoso!

Akata yeri

Arabambi Oko Oya

Alaafin ekun bu, a sa

Oloju Orogbo

Elereke obi

Eleyinju ogun'na

Olukoso lalu

Ina l'oju, ina l'enu

E'egun tin yona l'enu

Orisa ti n bologbo leru

San'giri, la'giri

Ola'giri Kankan figba edun bo.

A ri igba ota, sete

O fi alapa segunota

Ajisaye gbege oko Oya

Oloju Orogbo, Sango Olukosoooooo!

The translation for this is:

Sango the king of Koso,

The strong and mighty man.

Arabambi, husband of Oya.

The great and terrible ruler (of the palace) with a tiger.

The one with the eyes of bitter kola,

Whose cheeks are like kola nut.

Whose eyeballs are like coals of fire.

With fire in his eyes, and fire in his mouth.

The great masquerade that spits fire.

The god that is feared by all.

Sango the strong and mighty one.

With his might he reclaimed Edun.

He is unmoved by the sight of a thousand enemies.

He smites his enemies with his double-edged axe.

The one who awakens to impact the lives of all who call on him, the husband of Oya

The one whose eyes are like bitter kola, Sango - king of Koso.

General Notes on Sango

- Sango's sacred numbers are 4 and 6.

- Devotees always worship Sango on the fifth day of the week. This day is christened Ojo Jakuta, where Jakuta is a nickname for Sango.

- Sango is known in Santeria as Chango and is the most feared Orisha. Devotees in Palo call Sango Siete Rayos, while Haitians call him Ogou Chango.

- According to Candomble, Orisha Sango was the patron Orisha of slaves in the New World Plantations and was responsible for stirring them up into aggressive resistance.

- Bata gained popularity worldwide due to Sango and his devotees who dance solely to Bata.

- Sango leaves his mark on items by having them struck by lightning. When this happens, the item is moved to a shrine of Sango.

- Where an immovable item, e.g., a rock, is struck by lightning, Sango devotees convert the area around the item into a sacred site for worship.

Oya

Oya is the fearsome Orisha of wind, lightning, and violent storms. In a certain context, she is known as the goddess of death and rebirth. Oya, who is often called Iya Mesan (due to her giving birth to 9 stillborn children), was the beloved wife of Sango who participated in her husband's wars and ensured his victories in battle with her powers.

She is the Orisha of the River Niger that splits the Yoruba territory from the Hausa/Fulani territory of Northern Nigeria.

Being a fierce Orisha in her own rights, Oya, just like her husband, is a fierce warrior who wields a sword and is revered among Yoruba warriors. She is associated with the color red and has control over the dead.

According to Yoruba history, Oya loved her husband Sango greatly but was the cause of his downfall. In the Yoruba folklore, Oya hid Sango's sacred stones (the ones imbued with edun ara), so he would not act rashly toward her. She knew he needed them, and hiding them gave her some sort of respect from Sango. Her plan worked, and he carried her along on his military campaigns. However, as time progressed, it happened that Gbonka, a subordinate general, challenged Sango's authority – giving him an ultimatum to vacate the throne. Angered by the general, Sango sought his sacred stones and ax from Oya, only to discover that it was defiled with the blood of her menses. This was a bad time, and it only made Gbonka more daring as Sango didn't dole out instant judgment as he normally would. In a bid to put down the erring subordinate, Sango raised his ax to summon lightning, but the ax had been stripped of its power due to the "unclean" blood from Oya's menses.

When he realized that Oya was responsible for his shame – it was a taboo for warriors to leave a challenge unattended as that marked an acceptance of defeat, Sango left the palace in a fury to the place where he could restore the power of his ax and stones. His place of invocation, as it turned out, was a high rock facing the palace, and once he tried to restore the ax, he inevitably summoned lightning which struck the palace. Although some say it was a mistake, others say Sango intentionally struck the palace in anger as punishment to the people in the palace for watching while Gbonka's dare shamed him. Many died as the palace was ravaged by fire. Sango's two wives Oba and Osun, who lost their possessions in the fire, left the palace and returned to their homeland in anger and fear of Sango. In contrast, Oya, who realized her error and heard of Sango's demise, returned to her homeland in Nupe, where she drowned herself in the River Niger – also known as Odo Oya (River Oya).

Paths of Oya

139. Oya Iyansan

This is about the Niger River known in Yoruba as Odo-Oya and its nine tributaries. As a Storm Goddess, Oya is seen as the queen and source of the Niger River.

140. Oya Bomi

This path of Oya is known as a Storm Goddess and can manifest winds from a gentle breeze up to hurricane force level winds and tornadoes.

141. Oya Afefere

This path of Oya is the Goddess of Change, as seen in both nature and life. Oya's changes are known to bring about are not slow and gradual; they are fierce, quick, and often appearing destructive.

142. Oya Igbale

This path of Oya is known for securing the gates to cemeteries. Most notably, she protects graves marked with a cross.

143. Oya Obinidodo

This is the path of Oya that maintains contact with the ancestors.

144. Oya Ira

This path of Oya was said to have entered the lower realm of Ira in search of Sango when she heard about his death.

145. Oya Funke

This path of Oya guards and protects the unborn or stillborn children's spirit, taking them under her wing as she guides them to the afterlife.

146. Oya Iya Efon

This path of Oya can be invoked when an illness has become terminal.

147. Oya Dira

This path of Oya can be found in marketplaces where businesses are conducted. She is noted for being a very shrewd businesswoman and is also good with horses.

148. Oya De

This path of Oya was an unbeatable warrior whose skills were unmatched. After her death, she became deified as an Orisha.

149. Oya Nike

This path of Oya is known as the champion of women, as she often meted judgment on their behalf. Women often ask Oya to give them the ability to choose their words so they can speak persuasively and powerfully.

150. Oya Obinidodo

Oya's machetes represent the sword of truth, cutting quickly to the truth of the matter and dealing out matters of equality and custom. As an agent of change, Oya will cut through all injustices, deceits, and dishonesty in her path. She will speak only truths, even when they are hard to hear.

151. Oya Dumi

This path of Oya is known to be a strong and fierce protector of women. She also protects children and spouses.

Oriki Oya

Oya yeba, Iya mesan, Iya Oyo.

Orun afefe iku lele bioke,

Ayaba gbogbo le'ya obinrin.

Ogo mi ano gbogbo gbun,

Orisa mi abaya

Oya ewa, Iya mesan.

Ase.

Translation:

Spirit of the wind, Mother of nine, Mother of Oyo,

The winds of heaven bring down the ancestors,

You're the queen of all women.

Always protect me with your strong medicine,

My guardian Spirit is the queen.

Spirit of the Wind and Mother of Nine.

So, let it be.

General Notes on Oya

- Oya is generally known as Iya Mesan. In Candomble, she is called Oia.

- Orisha Oya is known for her passion shown by ravaging storms and winds.

- Oya is an Orisha who hides the secrets of the dead so that they can dwell in peace.

- For sacrifice, Oya accepts unseasoned akara'je, which is mashed beans fried in palm oil.

Chapter 8: Dark Orishas III: The Healers

Generally, the dark Orishas are known for judgment, often executed fiercely. This is unlike the white Orishas associated with calm and counsel – it is ideally a lot easier to listen when you don't have to worry about being struck down for a slight. As it has been stated earlier, there are certain Orishas who lie in-between the white and dark Orishas. In the same vein, a white Orisha can at other times act as rashly as a dark Orisha but will always revert to being calm and easy to entreat. Among these special categories of Orishas that lie in-between are the healers. Every Orisha has a specific sphere of influence aside from generally being able to express power. The healers are Orishas that specialize in healing, albeit possessing the power to influence other aspects of life.

Among the Orishas who are known for healing is Osanyin the Orisha, who knows all about plants and herbal medicine, Nana Buluku, who is the patroness of women – her healing virtues are mostly channeled toward women and Babaluwaye, who is the Orisha of all diseases. While Osanyin and Nana Buluku are of the white Orishas, Babaluwaye is of the dark Orishas and is prone to a temper. Some say that Babaluwaye being the Orisha of all diseases, doesn't just take away illness or heal sick people. He also inflicts terrible sicknesses, especially on people who err. His cult was noted for engaging in terrifying warfare where they inflicted sicknesses at will, both as a means of punishment and for selfish reasons.

Babaluwaye

Babaluwaye is one of the most feared Orishas in the Yoruba culture. He goes by many names, such as Babalu Aye, Obaluwaiye, and is said to be the son of Nana Buluku. At other times, he is depicted as the male path of Nana Buluku. Babaluwaye is the Orisha of life and death and is the patron Orisha of sicknesses. Babaluwaye operates in two major ways: he either cures the sick or doles out judgment by inflicting sickness. Despite medicines (modern or local) being available, should Babaluwaye strike a person, there is a greater probability of death – except when he is appeased.

According to Yoruba traditions, Babaluwaye is depicted as a man covered in sores, representing his control over leprosy and smallpox. Although muscular, Babaluwaye walks with crutches and is covered from head to toe in raffia curtains, used to hide the sores covering his body. He is often seen with two dogs who ease the pain of his sores by licking them constantly.

Based on his depiction, Babaluwaye is syncretized in Santeria with the Catholic Saint Lazarus, a known leper who was constantly seen with two dogs that licked his sores. In Santeria, Babaluwaye's day of celebration is held on the 17th of December in tandem with Saint Lazarus. In the same vein, he is associated with the number 17 and is mostly worshipped on Thursdays.

As the Orisha of diseases, Babaluwaye resides in a clay pot decked with cowrie shells. This pot is kept in a dark, calm place where he is not to be disturbed. Only his priest may invoke him using 18 cowrie shells placed on the clay pot. Should anyone try to summon Babaluwaye without being a priest, such a person risks becoming inflicted with terrible diseases leading to death.

According to Yoruba stories concerning Babaluwaye, he was initially a handsome prince revered by many. However, he was unruly – rather than respecting elder Orishas, he preferred to act on his own. Because of this, his attitude drew upon him different impurities scattered across the Yoruba realm. These impurities turned into sicknesses and diseases, which he eventually began traveling about with.

As he had been disfigured by impurities and was losing respect – even among his sons, Babaluwaye sought help from other Orishas, but none responded to him due to his track record of disrespect. Fortunately for him, Eshu, the Orishas messenger, took pity on him and brought him before Orunmila. Orunmila was not pleased with Babaluwaye's case and voiced his opinion to Eshu, saying, "You always bring me the hard ones, but I will speak to Ifa concerning him."

According to Ifa, Babaluwaye had been rejected due to his unruly and disobedient nature. However, Ifa told him he would be accepted and even celebrated in a strange land – he had already been exiled from home due to the impurities that stuck to him like scars. However, to get to the strange land, he would need to offer a sacrifice of grains (different types) and travel with a dog which was to be his companion at all times.

Babaluwaye, who had grown remorseful, appreciated Orunmila and acted as he was instructed. Helped by Eshu, he got the dog he needed and made his journey down to Dahomey. When he got there, he encountered a people with an unruly king that deemed himself a god and acted as he pleased. However, at the sight of Babaluwaye, the king fell to the ground and begged for forgiveness. It was as though he saw in Babaluwaye what would befall him if he continued in his unruly ways. He was prayed for by Babaluwaye, and he turned a new leaf to the relief of his people. Babaluwaye was greatly celebrated for his influence over the king and was seen as an emblem of consequences. When a person acts without caution or reason, there are bound to be consequences. Babaluwaye, who started as unruly, learned the hard way, but helped by Orunmila and Eshu, he overcame the consequences. He grew to become a gentle person with only his inner beauty and good character left. He was greatly disfigured on the outside due to the impurities he'd drawn toward himself. As the story goes, Babaluwaye ultimately became a king in Dahomey and ruled with wisdom.

Babaluwaye's Children

All devotees of Babaluwaye are known as his children. Each child of Babaluwaye specializes in healing - both spiritual and medical healing. Usually, they, just like Babaluwaye, have suffered one or more forms of skin disease in their younger years. As children of Babaluwaye, they possess both the ability to heal and the power to inflict terrible sickness on anyone who incurs their wrath. Usually, Babaluwaye's children are jovial but can easily switch to anger. Babaluwaye possesses fearsome powers, but that doesn't stop him from being calm - just as his children are joyful.

Invoking Babaluwaye

Babaluwaye, although a dark Orisha, is the one to call upon when faced with sicknesses - especially the terminal ones. As a healer, Babaluwaye knows whether to heal the sick or to allow a terminally sick person to pass on without pain. As with medical doctors who know when to recommend euthanasia - medically induced death due to terminal illnesses, Babaluwaye can help a sick person die in peace. This only happens when Babaluwaye himself has deemed the person's case as irredeemable - where death is inevitable. Where there is hope for survival, Babaluwaye would offer to heal as expected. A proof of his power to heal has been shown in the Yoruba legend where Sango was sick and could not be healed by any other. He visited Babaluwaye to heal him of his sickness, and he was promptly back to full health.

When invoking Babaluwaye, it is important to offer either roasted corn, black beans, dry grains, tobacco, or wine. He also welcomes meat sacrifices of vultures or other carcass-feeding birds. Place your offering before him on an altar decked with sacred stones and a statue of him. Yellow or purple candles are to be lit around the altar before you begin your prayer - strictly for mercy. For certainty and avoidance of error, have an experienced devotee do this on your behalf. The reason for this is that apart from the prayers, there will be a need for divination using either Diloggun or the Obi system of divination, and Babaluwaye only permits his own to invoke him.

To begin praying, it is expected that you begin with a recital such as this:

Babaluwaye, the god of all sicknesses and those who are sick.

I call upon you, have mercy on us.

We are your children, have mercy on us,

Keep sicknesses far away from our homes, and protect us - your children - from all plague.

Thank you, father, for you have answered, and you will heal us.

Paths of Babaluwaye

Babaluwaye has an average of 60 paths, with Sopona being one of his most fearsome paths. Sopona, which is the path that establishes him as the Orisha of smallpox, is rarely spoken of. This is done out of fear of being inflicted by smallpox, which was fatal in olden times, and out of reverence for Babaluwaye, with other paths more dignifying. He is best known as Babaluwaye, the father or king of the world, as this is more respectful and gives him a wider range of influence. However, here are a few paths of Babaluwaye:

152. Babaluwaye Asojano

This path of Babaluwaye speaks from Odu Ojuani, and he helps with warnings about impending famine, droughts, and epidemics. Some say that Asojano was disfigured when elders made use of unclean knives for his scarification ritual. Because of their error, Babaluwaye Asojano brought pestilence to the world. Asojano is the patron Orisha of persons treated unjustly.

153. Babaluwaye Asoyin Arara

This path of Babaluwaye is known as the father of the rain, which can kill due to its extremely hot temperature. This is the path that was said to have killed many with smallpox.

154. Babaluwaye Alua

This path of Babaluwaye is known for his wisdom

155. Babaluwaye Baba Arugbo

This is an aged path that appears as an elderly man – he is known as the ancient father.

156. Babaluwaye Afimaye

This path of Babaluwaye is known as the gravedigger and walks hand in hand with Orisha Oya, who rules over the dead.

157. Babaluwaye N'yone Nanu

This is a female path of Babaluwaye Asojano. She is always draped in black and dwells in ceiba trees.

158. Babaluwaye Molu

This is a path of Babaluwaye associated with hunting. He always makes use of a bow and arrow lined in leopard skin.

159. Babaluwaye Aberu Shaban

This is a male path of Babaluwaye, who eats intestines. He delivers food to the children of Babaluwaye Asojano

160. Babaluwaye Abokun

This is a male path of Babaluwaye and is identified as a farmer. He is known for fertilizing the earth and always walks with three companions, a lion, a crocodile, and the maja.

161. Babaluwaye Adu Kake

This is a path of Babaluwaye in Cuba and takes the form of a dog and lives naked in the mountains. He is said to possess a man's body with the head of a dog.

162. Babaluwaye Adan Wan

This is a male path of Babaluwaye, who kills anyone who offends him.

163. Babaluwaye Afrosan

This is a male path of Babaluwaye that uses the air for his activities.

164. Babaluwaye Afisinu Sanaje

This is a male path of Babaluwaye, who lives in the marketplace. He appears as a mouse and rarely speaks.

165. Babaluwaye Ajidenudo

This is another male path of Babaluwaye, who takes the form of a midget. He dwells with Osanyin and encourages witchcraft.

166. Babaluwaye Amabo

This is a male path of Babaluwaye, who inflicts offenders with chickenpox and elephantiasis.

167. Babaluwaye Apadado

This is a warrior path of Babaluwaye, who lives in anthills.

168. Babaluwaye Bayanana

This is a female path of Babaluwaye and is the patroness Orisha of virgin daughters of Babaluwaye Asojano.

169. Babaluwaye Ason'tuno

This is a male path of Babaluwaye and is known for traveling around with all diseases accompanying him.

Differences between Osanyin and Babaluwaye

At times, Osanyin is often misconceived as Babaluwaye due to the similarity of their office. However, both Orishas are different and operate in different ways. Among such differences are:

- Osanyin is strictly the Orisha of plants and herbal medicine, while Babaluwaye is the Orisha of sicknesses and diseases he can inflict or heal.

- Osanyin operates majorly via his staff of power, while Babaluwaye operates via his raffia curtains which he uses as a broom to sweep away sicknesses and disease.

- Osanyin heals without discrimination, but Babaluwaye's cult has been noted for inflicting sicknesses for selfish purposes. As such, they do not heal everyone – especially those upon whom they inflict sicknesses.

- Babaluwaye helps the terminally sick to pass on in peace, while Osanyin only applies plant medicine to help alleviate the pain of the sick.

- Babaluwaye is a dark Orisha possessing traits peculiar to white Orishas – he and his children are jovial. Osanyin, on the other hand, is a white Orisha.

Chapter 9: Talking to the Orishas With Diloggun

Communicating with the Orisha is possible. Orunmila ensured this when he taught mankind divination using the Ifa divination system. He gave select persons the means to commune with the Orishas, invoking their presence and powers over situations. But then, divination did not start with Orunmila and indeed started with Olodumare.

According to Yoruba legend, Olodumare summoned his children to a summit. Once they appeared before him and greeted him duly, Olodumare began speaking:

"My children, listen to me, for I am here to let you know things that must be. Know that my laws are yours to obey, and every task I give to you must be accomplished. I have borne you all for a purpose, which is to continue the work of creation I have started. I have finished my part, and all that is left is for you all to continue in my stead. You will continue to influence the growth of this planet I have created, and you will pave the way for those coming - the future generations.

Know that I will no longer take part in the growth of this planet, neither will I influence those on the planet. You will do all that for me. Your assignment will be to teach every living thing my will, my ways, and how they can reach out to me. First, they will come to you and report their case to you. Then, you will bring their requests to me so that I may tell you what to do for them. This is not a hard thing, but I must warn you - never try to carry out another person's assignment. You all have your assignments. Do them diligently, and don't try to carry out the assignment of any other.

Today, I give you the way to speak to me and teach those on the planet how to speak to me. Today, I give you Diloggun (16 cowrie shells) - use them as an oracle to speak to the people on the planet. Diloggun shall be your mouth to speak to all, telling them of my will in all cases."

Once Olodumare had spoken, he established how the Orishas could communicate with him first, then communicate within themselves, and last, how they should communicate with mankind. With Diloggun as a divination system, the power to recall the hidden past and tell the future's secrets was born in the Yoruba culture.

Types of Divination Systems

In Santeria, the divination system established by Olodumare is known as Diloggun. However, the Yoruba culture identifies this divination system as Odu Orisha Erindilogun, which signifies that it is a divination system of 16 cowrie shells. However, there are different forms of divination. Taking from the words of Olodumare when he said, "your assignment will be to teach every living thing my will, my ways and how they can reach out to me," notice this was a hint at each Orisha being able to divine. Osun has her means of divination, just like Orunmila has his means of divination - the widely recognized Ifa divination system. One thing, however, is common among the forms of divination, and that is that most utilize cowrie shells. Olodumare established divination using 16 cowrie shells, and how each Orisha utilizes these 16 cowrie shells determines the form of such divination.

Among the forms of divination known to the Yoruba religion are:

170. Diloggun

Diloggun is also known as Odu Orisha Erindilogun. Here, the 16 cowrie shells used for divination are only accessible to initiated priests (Santeros) and priestesses (Santeras) in the Yoruba Santerian religion. Only those who have been initiated and have gone through adequate training can read the 16 cowrie shells. With Diloggun, 256 signs can be read in the cowrie shells. Each sign comes with a unique parable or story attached to it. These parables are used to give counsel and determine the course of a person's life. The past, present, and future are laid bare during readings, and once counsel is given, it is left to the individual to act upon such counsel. The Diloggun is very similar to the Ifa divination system.

171. Odu Ifa

Odu Ifa refers to a collection of prayers and stories passed down by Orunmila to his priests and priestesses, who likewise pass down the knowledge from generation to generation. In Odu Ifa, 16 major books are subdivided into 16 minor books of secrets. There are 256 Odu in this divination system, and they hold the solution to all possible circumstances. With Odu Ifa, there is a divining accuracy of at least 90%, and with it, counsel and wisdom can be given concerning any circumstance brought before Ifa.

172. Obi

This divination system makes use of five pieces of kola nuts. The pieces are thrown onto a divining cloth, and a divining priest or priestess reads the signs they display. To a considerable extent, it is deemed as one of the easiest forms of divination among the three.

General Notes on Divination

Divination is a sacred tradition in the Yoruba culture that helps to determine a person's fate. This isn't based on just foretelling of the future but also calling into account the past's deeds via divine hindsight. Once the past and present have been laid bare, the future can then be foretold accurately.

Consequent to the fact that divination is a sacred art, only experienced devotees, priests, and priestesses of the Orishas are permitted to engage in it. Santeria does not allow a non-initiate to practice Diloggun. The knowledge of divining in Santeria is closely guarded so that only generic information is offered to inquisitive minds - but secrets are only known by initiates being trained to practice Diloggun. In the same vein, the Obi system of divination and Odu Ifa strictly warn that only an experienced devotee is to engage in divination. The reason is not farfetched - there are many possibilities (256), and not all those possibilities are good. Negative possibilities can occur, and it takes an experienced mind to be clear of such possibilities. Also, there is a greater chance of misreading the signs seen in divination when done by an amateur, let alone a non-initiate. Hence, to avoid errors and possible terror, it is advised that a person gets initiated and is duly taught before engaging in any divination systems. Likewise, you can seek the assistance of a practicing diviner rather than risk error and its attendant consequences.

Tools for Divination

Diloggun being a divination system of cowrie shells, require certain things to be in place before any divination can be done. By default, it is expected that an Oba - the general name given to divining priests and priestesses of Santeria, possess a bag of cowrie shells to be used for divination. Sixteen cowrie shells are used for divination, but the Oba must possess up to 21 cowrie shells. When divining for Eshu the Orishas messenger, 21 cowrie shells are expected to be in his possession. In comparison, 18 cowrie shells are expected to be in his possession when divining for other Orishas.

173. Divining Bone

Aside from the cowrie shells used in divination, a small bone is required to help read the shells' signs. This bone symbolizes the dividing line between good and bad, and because of this, it is essential to every divination attempt.

174. Divining Platform

Diloggun is a divination system that specializes in throwing down cowrie shells and then reading the signs made by them. However, the shells are not to be thrown in any manner. Neither are they to be thrown just anywhere. It is expected that the cowrie shells or kola nuts are thrown onto a divining platform for all forms of divination. This could either be a cloth - which is mostly white, a table, wooden tray, or a raffia mat.

175. Divining Cloth

For every divination system, there is sacred clothing worn before any attempt at divination. Like the divining cloth used as a platform, an Oba is adorned in white clothing - while in other contexts, the cloth worn is red. The divining cloth worn is often decked with cowrie shells and is blessed as a form of consecration to the Orishas before it is used/worn. Diviners are expected to be shed of any items such as a ring or other jewelry, as these would impair the accuracy of their divination.

176. Efun

This is a ball made of powdered eggshells held in the palm. It represents Ire (blessing) in divination.

177. Ota

This is a black rocky item that fits into the palm. It represents Ofo (misfortune) in divination.

178. Cleansing

Generally, the tools used for divination are cleansed and consecrated via prayers and a blood sacrifice. This ensures that all impurities are washed out of the items, leaving them clean to be used by the Orishas for responding to mankind.

179. Timing of Divination

Divining only happens from dawn until the early hours of dusk. It is believed that Osun, who is a principal Orisha of divination, leaves divining once it is dusk and only returns to it once the day breaks. Hence, for accuracy, it is advised to divine before dusk.

Intention in Divination

Recalling a lesson from Orisha Ogun, who turned his back on the people he swore to protect due to their carelessness in invoking him, it stands to reason that the Orishas respond only to sincerity. Trying to invoke the Orishas for fun is a risky gamble and, at the same time, a futile endeavor as they would usually not respond. No matter how serious a case, the Orishas will not respond where it is perceived there is an iota of insincerity or lack of seriousness. Where intent is in doubt, the Orishas have no business responding.

The intention is important both to the diviner and the person requesting divination. The diviner must, first of all, be pure and likewise ready to divine - receive the counsel of the Orishas for such divination to be accurate. Where a diviner is impure or not ready, the cowrie shells will fall into indiscernible patterns until the diviner has done the needful preparation. In this case, preparation isn't just outwardly displayed but is also a matter of the heart or sincere intent.

In the same vein, a person requesting divination must prove to be sincere and willing to carry out the Orishas' instructions and must not lie to the diviner - lying is tantamount to insincerity. Where a client is insincere or has no plan of abiding by the Orishas' counsel, such a client will get no response from the Orishas. Thus, it would be a waste of effort and time to the diviner and the client. Due to the uncertainty surrounding people's intent, priests are asked if clients are willing to obey the Orishas before they progress further into divining with the cowrie shells.

Chapter 10: Understanding What the Shell Mouths Say

Every Yoruba inclined religion engages in divination - it is foundational to the entire religion and serves as the basis for moral principles. Yoruba people, in general, depend greatly on what the Orishas say before making decisions. Among the devotees, certain people are selected to undergo sacred training for a while before they're permitted to invoke the Orishas via divination.

Although a great deal of knowledge about divination is kept sacred within the confines of cults dedicated to the Orishas, there is still sufficient knowledge available to the public. All knowledge about divination was initially sacred, and no person outside the cult could learn or know the ways of divination. However, as the years progressed into recent times, some elders - devotees with great experience in divining deemed it fit to make certain knowledge known about divination. This was done to preserve the knowledge of divination and garner interest in the Orisha tradition. Westernization brought about a wind of extinction that threatened to erase the Yoruba people's history, culture, and religion. First, it began with slavery and oppressive regimes, but over time a new strategy has played out, and it is none other than distracting the newer generations with the thrills of foreign cultures.

The aim of preserving Yoruba tradition was largely achieved. But it didn't end there. Aside from preserving the ancient traditions, this sacred knowledge gave power to interested people so that they could rightly divine and determine the course of their personal lives without having to call on a priest. Of course, it is advised that a priest is consulted for divination of greater accuracy, but it doesn't hurt to be able to foretell one's own destiny - even if it's just surface information.

What the Shell Mouths Say

Cowrie shells have always been of great value in the Yoruba culture since their inception. Aside from being used as money in the olden times, it remained a vital tool of divination. To some, the cowrie shells serve as the third eye to gain access into the realm of divinities and our ancestors. This is a timeless realm filled with endless knowledge and wisdom that can help us live with greater fulfillment. With the cowrie shells, we gain access into all ages; the past, present, and future.

According to Yoruba tradition, the cowrie shells serve as the Orishas' voice, and they speak uniquely. To make them speak, the cowrie shells are gently tossed onto a divining platform. Depending on how they fall and the pattern they create, the diviner then reads their interpretation based on sacred knowledge about the cowrie shells' patterns.

Recalling the types of divination, the interpretation is given to the patterns made by the cowrie shells differ. For instance, the Obi system of divination interprets the fallen patterns as either "yes" or "no," while the Diloggun system of divination gives more than just "yes" or "no" interpretations.

Obi Divination

In the Obi system of divination, kola nuts are used in place of cowrie shells, and questions are thrown to the oracle in ways that would generate a "yes" or "no" response. For instance, a person could ask, "Will I prosper if I do this?" rather than "What should I do?" This way, the oracle recognizes the free will and intent of a divining client. Where questions are put straightforwardly, it becomes easy for the oracle to respond appropriately.

In the Obi system of divination, four pieces of kola nuts are traditionally used, and their fallen patterns are placed into five categories. However, diviners of the Obi system in the United States utilize cowrie shells in place of kola nuts, but the interpretation strategy is the same.

The four shells or kola nuts represent the secrets of the past and the future. Here, the diviner places the shells in his/her hand and prays over the question you've posed. Free praying, the diviner then blows into the shells and tosses them onto the divining cloth or table and interprets the pattern shown. Where there is uncertainty about an interpretation, the whole exercise is repeated.

The five categories of interpretation are defined as follows:

1. Alaafia

Four shell mouths facing up; as the name implies, it is the response of peace and certainty. It is the oracle saying "yes" to your question. When this happens, your heart's desires may be granted a lot faster than expected. While this is a solid guarantee, you're expected to make one more toss of the shells to confirm the first response. You're expected to see a second alaafia as proof.

2. Etawa

Three shell mouths face up, while one shell mouth faces down; this is an undecided response. It is a "maybe" due to the existence of one shell contradicting three others. Etawa could also be considered as a "yes," albeit shaky. Hence, it is expected to make another throw to get a more decisive answer.

3. Ejife

Two shell mouths face down, while two shell mouths face down; this is also a solid "yes" due to the balance between the shells. Here, there is no need for a confirmatory throw.

4. Okanran

One shell mouth faces up, while three shell mouths face down; this is a firm "no" as three shells contradict one. This indicates that there is a great deal of work to do before success is achieved.

5. Oyekun

Four shell mouths face down; this represents total darkness. It is the strongest "no" and requires a ritual cleansing to churn out the negative energies surrounding the matter you tabled before the oracle.

Diloggun Divination

The cowrie shells in Diloggun are consecrated through blood sacrifice and possess deeper meanings than the kola nuts used in the Obi system of divination. Diloggun, a variant of Odu Erindilogun, is practiced in Santeria and requires initiation before anyone can learn the rudiments of divining with the shells.

To get started divining, a diviner is expected to give praises to Olodumare, Egun, and the ancestors first. Once this is done, Elegba, the messenger path of Eshu, is to be invoked alongside the Orisha that is to be consulted, e.g., Osun. An offering must be in place before going further to appease Elegba and the Orisha you're consulting. Note that the offering must be specific to the consulted Orisha - don't give an offering meant for Yemoja to Ogun; it's a grievous error. It is expected that you give a part of every offering to Elegba so he can keep the channel between you and your Orisha open.

Once a diviner is done the needful in giving praises and offerings, attention must be paid to the pattern in which the cowrie shells fall. In Diloggun, the patterns of the shell are classed into two-parent Odu and composite Odu. The parent Odu appears after the first toss of the shells, while the composite Odu appears after the second toss. Both Odu makes up the overall pattern of the shells and is to be interpreted as one. For instance, where the first toss produces five as the parent Odu, and the second toss produces nine as the composite Odu, the pattern made is 5-9. This is then to be interpreted either as a blessing or misfortune.

To get the interpretation, the tools known as Efun and Ota are used. Both items are placed in the divining client's hands, who then shakes his hands and divides both items into separate hands. Both hands are to be firmly closed until the diviner asks the client to unveil the left or right hand.

Once the diviner has read the pattern, the numbers will determine which hand is to be opened. If the Efun is revealed, the interpretation veers toward blessings, but the interpretation is nothing but misfortune if the Ota is unveiled. However, divining doesn't end there. Inquiries have to be made to determine the source of either the blessings or the misfortunes. Here, the diviner would have to converse with the client and interpret to arrive at a conclusion. Once the source of either blessing or misfortune is revealed, the diviner would then make further inquiries to determine what sacrifice or offering is to be made either in thanksgiving or plea for mercy.

Each Odu is represented by the number of shells that face up after falling onto the divining platform. Hence, where ten shells fall face up, the Odu is equal to ten. There are 16 basic patterns or parent Odu that could be read from each throw of the cowrie shells. However, underneath these 16 patterns are 256 composite Odu that could be read. The 16 basic patterns include:

- **Okanran** – A single shell mouth faces up; it means hurt no one

- **Eji Oko** – Two shell mouths face up; it means feel no hate nor seek destruction for others

- **Eta Ogunda** – Three shell mouths face up, it means seek no vengeance

- **Irosun** – Four shell mouths face up, it means do not slander nor trap anyone

- **Ose** – Five shell mouths face up, it means avoid envy toward anyone and anything

- **Obara** – Six shell mouths face up, it means do not lie

- **Odi** – Seven shell mouths face up, it means do not be corrupt neither should you corrupt anyone

- **Eji Onile** – Eight shell mouths face up; it means to respect the secrets of others and use your head wisely

- **Osa** – Nine shell mouths face up; it means to avoid being fake with others

- **Ofun** – Ten shell mouths face up, it means do not steal, curse or swear falsely

- **Owanrin** – Eleven shell mouths face up, it means do not kill or ruin other people's lives and be grateful for good done to you

- **Ejila Sebora** – Twelve shell mouths face up; it means avoid tragedies and scandals

- **Eji Ologbon** – Thirteen shell mouths face up, this is also known as metala, and it means to respect the ancestors

- **Ika** – Fourteen shell mouths face up, it is also known as merinla, and it means do not spread corruption, evil, or disease

- **Ogbegunda** – Fifteen shell mouths face up, also known as marunla and means respect the elders, children, father, and mother

- **Alaafia** - Sixteen shell mouths face up, it is known as merindilogun, and it means that if you listen to this counsel, you will find peace and boldness when standing before Olodumare.

- **Opira** - This is the seventeenth pattern where no mouth faces up, and it means the reading is inaccurate. This could be the fault of either the diviner or the client.

Conclusion

Diloggun as a means of divination provides insight into a person's life and can help redefine destiny. It is a means of communication with the Orishas who have existed before creation and will remain even after this world's end. The Yoruba people believe in a proverb that says, *"What an elder sees whilst seated, a young man cannot see even if he stands at the peak of the highest mountain."* The Orishas have existed before time. It is only wise that they're sought for their counsel and power – after all, they are the ancient ones whose wisdom and powers transcend our space and time.

Here's another book by Mari Silva that you might like

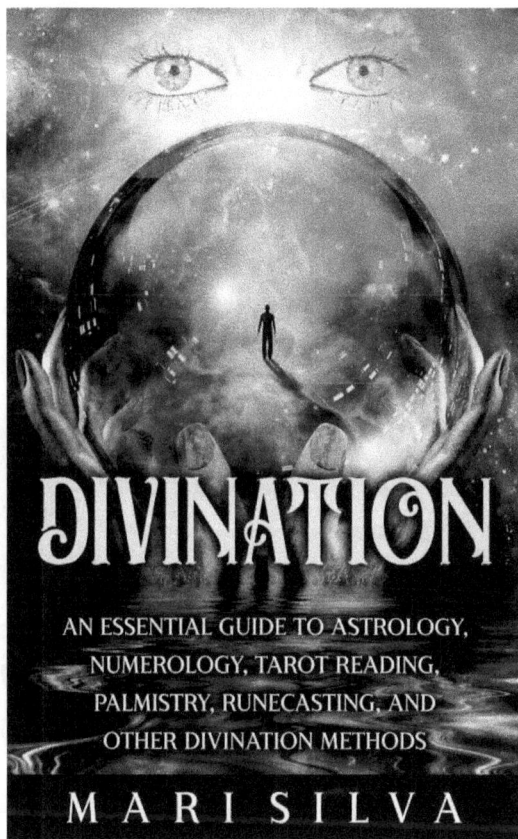

Your Free Gift (only available for a limited time)

Thanks for getting this book! If you want to learn more about various spirituality topics, then join Mari Silva's community and get a free guided meditation MP3 for awakening your third eye. This guided meditation mp3 is designed to open and strengthen ones third eye so you can experience a higher state of consciousness. Simply visit the link below the image to get started.

https://spiritualityspot.com/meditation

References

Falola, Toyin (2016) | Encyclopedia of the Yoruba

J. Omosade Awolalu | Yoruba Beliefs & Sacrificial Rites

Adeoye C.L. (1989) | Igbagbo ati Esin Yoruba

William Bascom | Sixteen Cowries

Idowu E.B. (1962) | Olodumare; God in Yoruba Belief

Harold Courlander | Tales of Yoruba Gods & Heroes

Lynch, Patricia Ann (2018) | African Mythology, A to Z

William Bascom (1991) | Ifa Divination: Communication Between Gods and Men in West Africa

Ifaloju A. | Iwori Meji; Ifa Speaks on Righteousness

James J. Kulevich | The Odu of Lucumi; Information on all 256 Odu Ifa

Fagbemijo Amosun Fakayode (2012) | Ori Mi Gbe Mi; Ori Support Me

Makinde M.A. (1985) | A Philosophical Analysis of the Yoruba Concepts of Ori and Human Destiny

Ifaloju A. (2007) | Ori – The Divine Container of Destiny, Character & Potential, Seed of the Creator

Elebuibon, Yemi; Adventures of Obatala

James T. Houk (1995) | Spirits, Blood, and Drums; the Orisha Religion of Trinidad

John Mason | Orin Orisa; Songs for Selected Heads

Robert Marcel (1997) | Ogun Worship in Idanre; Iron and Identity in a Yoruba Town

Adeoye C.L. (1989) |Igbagbo ati Esin Yoruba

Robert D. Pelton (1989) | The Trickster in West Africa; A Study of Mythic Irony and Sacred Delight

Alamoja Yoruba (2019) | Esu is Not Satan; Who Esu Is and Who He Is Not

Murrell, Nathaniel S. (2009) | Afro-Caribbean Religions; An Introduction to Their Historical, Cultural and Sacred Traditions.

Monaghan (2014) | Encyclopedia of Goddesses and Heroines

Akalatunde, Osunyemi (2005) | Ona Agbani; The Ancient Path – Understanding and Implementing the Ways of Our Ancestors

Chief Yagbe Awolowo Only (2016) | Deities and Divination

The Yoruba Religious Concepts; Understanding the Belief Concepts of the Lucumi Faith

"African Poems – Oral Poetry from Africa." Africanpoems.net

"HERITAGE: Be Mindful of Your Self-Talk = It's a Conversation with the Universe..." Chief Yagbe Awolowo Onilu, yagbeonilu.com.

"Ọmọ Oòduà." Ọmọ Oòduà, ooduarere.com.

"OWULAKODA Blog." OWULAKODA Blog, owulakoda.wordpress.com.

www.ingramcontent.com/pod-product-compliance
Lightning Source LLC
Chambersburg PA
CBHW071900090426
42811CB00004B/689